What is Communi

Other *What is . . .?* books available

Linguistics
Psychology
Accounting
Social Anthropology

in preparation

Engineering
Religious Studies
Business Studies

What is Communication Studies?

James Watson

Senior Lecturer in Communication Studies and Education
West Kent College of Further Education

Edward Arnold

© James Watson 1985

First published in Great Britain 1985 by
Edward Arnold (Publishers) Ltd, 41 Bedford Square, London
WC1B 3DQ

Edward Arnold (Australia) Pty Ltd, 80 Waverley Road,
Caulfield East, Victoria 3145, Australia

Edward Arnold, 300 North Charles Street, Baltimore, Maryland
21201, U.S.A.

British Library Cataloguing in Publication Data

Watson, James, *1936—*
    What is communication studies?
    1. Communication——Study and teaching (Higher)
    ——Great Britain   2. Communication——Study and teaching
    (Secondary)——Great Britain
    I. Title
    001.51′07′1141   P91.5.G7

    ISBN 0–7131–6447–6

Text set in 10/11pt Times Compugraphic
by Colset Private Ltd., Singapore.
Printed and bound by Richard Clay
(The Chaucer Press) Limited,
Bungay, Suffolk.

Contents

Preface

Whatever we think of the new language of computers, one phrase from its terminology deserves a blessing: user-friendly. It is a comforting expression. It indicates that, despite all the complications of the hard and software of computers, the user is to be considered in a kindly fashion. That, too, is how a brief introduction to communication studies ought to be – user-friendly. The users I envisage are students aged between 16 and 18, contemplating trying something new and selecting 'A' level Communication Studies as an option, students at school or in further education who are studying communication in some form or another – on courses leading to Business and Technician Education (BTEC) diplomas, the City and Guilds' Communication Skills Level 2 certificate or other communication and media studies certificates. Would-be undergraduates thinking about a degree course in communication, media or film studies may also wish to dip into this volume.

What is Communication Studies? is not intended to be the 'textbook nobody should be without'. Rather it is designed to take the reader to a vantage point above the landscape of communication studies as it has evolved over recent years, to indicate the contours of such a landscape, the chief features. In Chapter 1 I have tried to define the nature of this essentially interdisciplinary subject and the kind of response it requires from the student. Indeed I have laid special stress on student response because the subject requires a high degree of self-awareness, question-asking and reflection as well as a capacity for independent study. Because it is such a vast field of study, communication studies obliges us to structure our learning, make it containable. In Chapter 2 I suggest ways in which this can be done by establishing clear aims, by relating application to these aims and by using theory in order to clarify and reinforce those aims. A final section in this chapter cites issues as representing a useful means of focusing on content. By this time I think we will be ready, hopefully in a user-friendly manner, to explore in Chapter 3, some of the terms students will encounter and be expected to use during their course. Only what I consider to be centrally important terms are explained and illustrated here, though throughout the book the basic vocabulary of communication studies is used regularly and in varying contexts. Chapter 4 outlines skills the student will be expected to develop – the ability to assimilate, comprehend and organize material and ideas, to identify a suitable audience for each act of communication and select an appropriate form of presentation. Communication Studies is a *doing* subject. This does not mean repeating skills exercises slavishly as ends in themselves; it suggests that students *apply* learning, experience and theory in order to develop a deeper understanding of human communication. Appendix A suggests further reading on communication and media studies topics, and includes *A Dictionary of Communication and Media Studies*, by Watson and Hill, which may be useful in explaining further the terminology used here. Appendix B gives details of higher education courses in communication, media and film studies in the United Kingdom, an area of provision which has expanded dramatically in recent years. In Appendix C I have provided a summary of the Associated Examining Board's A Level in Communication Studies, and included a typical case study.

I have not attempted to connect up into a syllabus-style sequence the elements of communication studies. 'Routes of study' depend upon particular course aims and objectives; who is doing the learning; whether this learning is based in school, college, polytechnic or university; whether communication studies is rigorously examinable or whether it is classified as a general support subject in a wider curriculum. And much depends upon available resources, upon the time allowed for the subject and – not least – upon the teacher. Whatever the sequencing of elements for study, a communication studies syllabus ought to take into account that there is probably most to be learnt where different areas of knowledge and experience interconnect.

Dividing the subject into lists of topic headings is probably unavoidable, especially if more than one teacher is involved. The danger is that interconnections or links will be blurred or go unperceived. If students sense a 'missing link' in the coherence of their studies, it is their responsibility to themselves and their teachers to speak up immediately. The more questions students ask of their teachers, the better: questions are indicators of learning progress, not ignorance.

1

What is Communication Studies and why choose to study it?

'Why communicate?' might at first be considered a damnfool question. One could just as well ask – why breath? We do it, and that's that. Indeed if we spent too much time thinking about our breathing we might forget how to do it: and that could seriously injure our health. Equally it might be argued that thinking too hard about the processes of communication could hinder our proficiency by making us too self-conscious of the mechanics. We may end up like someone who has stripped down a motor cycle but cannot quite stick the pieces together again to get the machine back on the road. Yet in many ways the study of communication serves as an antidote to over-concentration upon the 'parts' of learning and experience. It comprises the broadest of landscapes. The flow and diversity of communication is too interlinked, too interdependent to permit the blinkered view. For example, when a person addresses us, if we concentrate merely on the words being spoken we are less likely to grasp the full meaning of a message than if we observe *how* those words are expressed. We watch the communicator's eyes, facial expression, hand and body movements – cues which will assist us in reading the message.

The process is more complex than it seems at first. It is also fascinating because we discover how much of ourselves – of our perceptions and experience – is involved in the interpreting of the message. Even our sense of uncertainty has value – uncertainty whether we are reading the person and the message correctly, whether we have misread the cues or signs. In fact the ultimate fascination in studying interpersonal communication is its mystery: can we ever be sure that we have understood a message or conveyed a message as we intended?

Communication Studies may be usefully classified as a process of exploration, and it is one for which all students are already well equipped, though they may not at first realize this.

Process-centred

Most academic subjects are information-centred. There is a body of knowledge which has to be absorbed before that knowledge can be acted upon. This gives teachers a great advantage over their students who can only begin to assert their own views on the subject once the necessary facts have been assimilated. In communication studies the relationship between the student and the subject, and the student and the teacher is arguably of a different order. Facts are important, but perception of those facts is open to debate: a teacher's perception of a situation may be different from a student's; it may be more articulate in its expression, but it is not incontrovertibly better or right. The teacher's view of the media, of TV news, of the impact of advertising on audiences, of the popularity of the latest television soap opera, may well be based on a more considered judgement of the evidence, but the case still has to be pressed home through argument, and students retain the right to differ. There are instances when a student's view of certain communicative situations may be better informed than that of the teacher: students could well know more about the thinking behind the styles of dress, modes of popular music, patterns of youth group behaviour than their teachers. Having the occasional upper-hand on the teacher is good for student morale.

Communication studies is anything but a 'sit down, open your books and listen to me' mode of learning. At its best it is a multi-way discourse between students and teacher where the students have an enormous store of personal experience to draw upon – experience which they will have to learn to link to new information, to test against the experience and knowledge of the teacher and of other students. In dealing with such vital elements of the communication process as feelings, opinions, perceptions and values, no teacher can lay down the law. Thus the communication studies teacher tends to act as a facilitator of learning: helping to pose the questions rather than answer them; suggest lines of enquiry rather than offer solutions; provide source material, guidance and clarification rather than impose solutions. This is not to say that the teacher steps down altogether from the role of evaluator. The task of the teacher remains one of ensuring, vigilantly, the logical argument, the fair and thorough use of information in supporting such argument, of shaping the learning process in ways that will enable students to develop their own powers of evaluation.

A challenge

Initially students could well find the gift of greater independence which communication studies confers difficult to handle. Such questions as, 'What do *you* think about it?' 'How do *you* perceive it?' 'How does your own experience match up with what we are studying?' can come as a shock. In schools we are used to being told what to think. We are also conditioned into believing education is always about deciphering what is good from what is bad: 'Is Poem A superior to Poem B? – give reasons for your judgement'.

In communication studies we do not shrink from evaluation. Well-practised critical faculties are as essential in the subject as in any other, but the 'bad' is never rejected as being beneath our interest, because the inferior as well as the superior may be a clue to greater understanding; a clue to meaning. Communication students are encouraged to be attentive to all message systems, however trivial they may seem to be. Not only great literature, but films and television programmes form material for study. Comics, cartoons, posters, photographs, even cigarette cards constitute rich sources of evidence. The ways in which people dress, do their hair, embellish their gardens, homes, cars, offices are indicators of what people want to say about themselves and often what they wish to remain unsaid. New to such 'liberties' some students might well suffer from a crisis of confidence or even of identity. They find they have to substantially relinquish the security of a body of facts for the uncertainty of a process of learning in which thinking for themselves is of paramount importance.

Identifying three phases of progress This challenge usually comes at a tricky time in the student's own personal growth.[1]

[1] Explained at length by W.G. Perry in *Forms of intellectual and ethnic development in the college years: a scheme* (USA: Holt, Rinehart and Winston, 1970).

The development of the post-school student passes through three major phases. The first of these is called *dualism*. This means that the student tends to see things in very simple black and white terms, of right and wrong. Eventually, in the *relativist* stage, the student recognizes that there are different shades of opinion and legitimate uncertainties; in short, that the world is more complex, life more complicated than allowed for in the dualist stage. Here students gingerly accept the possibility that views other than their own may have truth in them. Such a realization may lead forward into the third stage, that of *commitment*, where students are sufficiently confident to grasp new ideas, to incorporate them in their own scheme of things, or life view, and possibly to act upon them.

It is not an inevitable process; alternatives to growth can show themselves in three ways: retreat; temporizing (playing for time); or escape, see Fig. 1. Faced with the prospect of the insecurity that comes from realizing that nothing in terms of ideas and values is absolutely certain, students might retreat (as many adults do, whether they are students or not) into the absolute phase of dualism. Communication students will soon be able to recognize that dualist behaviour often results in *defensive* or *deflective* communication, used to protect an oversimplified, dogmatic view of the world from alternative perception and argument. It shows itself in people becoming deaf to what they do not want to hear, blind to what they do not want to see.

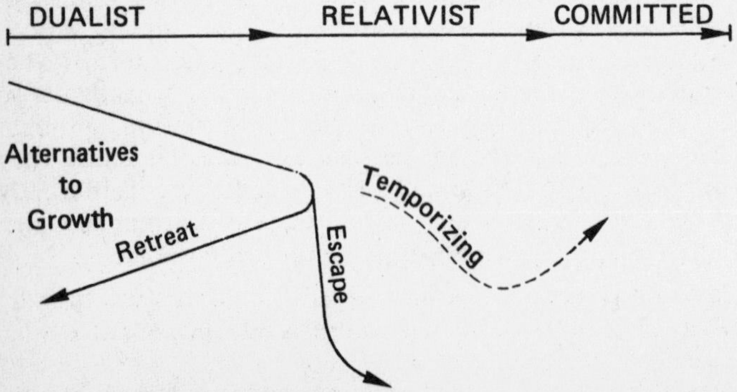

Fig. 1   Phases of development

Temporizing may be a state you will recognize from your own experience. You put one toe into the cold sea of new experience and withdraw it again. You might pad along the sand for a while; even open a dialogue with yourself, debating whether to have another try. This *intrapersonal* communication constitutes a clamour of soundless voices and opinions, arising from current observation and past experience.

The debate at the water's edge may also receive exterior stimulus. When a friend calls, 'Stick you foot in, you coward!' *interpersonal* communication has begun. Or if a teacher says, 'I know you can do it', you may summon up the courage and the confidence to test the water more fully. That is growth. You risk the uncertain. You advance towards maturity. That is what education is largely about, and the study of communication necessarily involves some study of human intellectual development.

Traversing boundaries

As well as an understanding of likely stages of development, an appreciation of the nature of the subject itself is needed. Earlier I described it as a process-centred discipline. It is equally person-centred. Even when we are examining mass communication we must keep in clear focus the role of people as individuals; otherwise we plunge into dangerous generalizations, of *massification*, where humanity is regarded as if it were made up entirely of sheep or robots. Though the media may stereotype people in this way, communication students must resist such easy and convenient classification, at the same time studying why and how stereotyping takes place.

Most subjects which you will have studied at school or college will have had fairly sharply defined boundaries. The headings in the syllabuses are clear: Tudor Britain, the Victorian novel, and so on. By its very nature, communication cannot so readily be slipped into a neat pigeon hole. It flows through and over boundaries. It is an interdisciplinary subject. Of course communication studies does have identifiable territories (see Chapter 2) but these are so interlinked and interdependent that to categorize them would be to seriously impede understanding. Being so interdisciplinary, communication studies is the ultimate poacher; it draws its material, its evidence and many of its theories from a wide range of fields of study, including psychology, sociology, linguistics, history, economics, politics, telecommunications and anthropology.

That is part of its difficulty, but also of its value and interest. In a sense, communication studies is especially concerned with the connections between disciplines and areas of knowledge, in the *interface*.

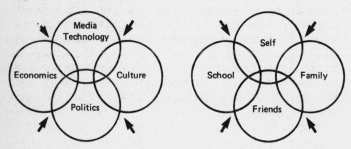

Fig. 2   Fig. 3

The arrows in Fig. 2 indicate the points of contact, of overlap, where interaction takes place. The study of communication is very much involved with the analysis of what happens to the processes of communication both within the circles and where they join and how those processes exert an influence. Fig. 3 illustrates interest in a more localized interaction.

We might wish to explore not only the interaction between ourselves and others, but the relationships between the many roles we all have to play in our everyday life, as in Fig. 4.

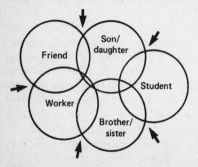

Fig. 4

We will probably discover, for example, that where the role boundaries meet or overlap there can be difficulties, *role strain*; when we have to play two contradictory roles at once, for example, such as when a teacher has his or her own child in class as a pupil.

Role strain is a common experience, and experience is as much a part of the material of communication studies as book-learning. Evidence of communication is all around us. We need to look for it, to think about it and sooner or later we will need to organize it, to systematize it. While we must accept that each individual person is unique, and that each act of communication is unique, we would make no progress unless we were searching for shapes and patterns, if we were not attempting to elicit some kind of meaning from the profusion of data available to us.

Hargreaves (see Appendix A, p. 73) says, 'Although each individual is indeed unique he does possess certain characteristics which he shares in common with all other individuals. Further, human behaviour is, within limits, regulated in a number of ways . . . [it] takes place within structured situations and it is very doubtful whether we can say much about the unique individual unless we can analyse the structures

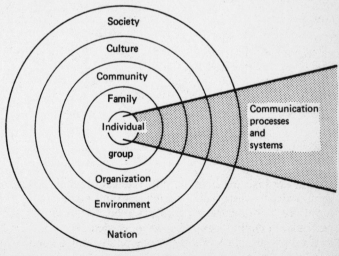

Fig. 5

within which such a person thinks, feels and acts'. Communication studies sets out to explore process within structure, see Fig. 5.

Once again, we are investigating connections – how the individual interacts with the wider structure of family life, how that interaction is influenced by the community which in turn is the product of culture and environment.

Fig. 5, and what has been said so far, indicate that communication studies is very much a subject of the here and now. It is a contemporary study concerned with today's culture in today's world, with what is happening this minute between individuals, in groups, in communities, in organizations, across nations. What is being said, what is being published in the press, broadcast or shown on the cinema screen is the currency of the subject. However, none of the above has sprung instantly into existence. Everything which exists has a history. It has come from somewhere, it has evolved, has been influenced in its growth by many factors, and it is this, the historical or developmental perspective, which must now be added to our model (Fig. 6).

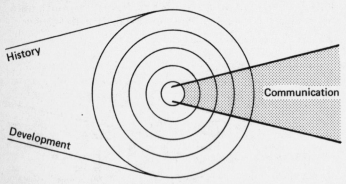

Fig. 6

I am not insisting here that all students of communication should also be historians, though it would not do them any harm. Yet it is essential for students to be alert to the fact that each act of communication has its antecedent. If the members of a family are not speaking to one another, if a newspaper appears with a blank space on its front page, if a country forbids certain minority languages to be taught in the nation's schools, the investigator must probe the past.

Communication studies students need to become good detectives, weighing the evidence, looking for cues, searching beyond formal or official explanations; we are not concerned with facts alone, but the factors which colour those facts – feelings, opinions, perceptions, beliefs, values, all the while aware that there are those with privileged access to the means of communication, with control over them. Indeed we must be aware at all times that, as far as mass communication is concerned, the means of communication constitute part of the apparatus of influence and control in every society. Thus, linked in with the historical dimension of the subject is the political one. Communication is influence, it is power; therefore communication, especially where it reaches people in large numbers, is politics – the study of the way power is distributed and exerted and of how decisions are made.

It follows that we also need to familiarize ourselves with economics, the way 'money talks' and the role played in society by large organizations in influencing and sometimes monopolizing message systems. Of equal interest to us are other organizations or groups whose business is not production or trade, but ideas – pressure groups, for example, employing communication as a means to preserve, change or overturn the way things are. We are interested not only in how such groups use communication systems to attain their goals, but what happens, communication-wise, within those groups – the *dynamics* of the group.

Practice and experience

Application aids understanding: practice builds confidence; confidence is likely to improve competence, and both help to create a solid base for future exploration. This explains why many teachers view communication studies not only as a process and person-centred subject but one which may be described as task-orientated. You *do* in order to learn. Experience – activity, practice, trying things out – enables students to develop that precious quality, insight. This, I would argue, is of greater value in our studies than expertise. While it is difficult to deny that in order to understand the communication process a person needs to try it out, expertise is not the major objective. In many activities expertise often indicates a capacity to do something without thinking about it. Conscious learning may have ceased and automatic pilot may have taken over.

This condition is not what 'learning by doing' aspires to, though we might usefully discuss the implications of expertise that has gone beyond the point of reflection. Where along the line, we might ask, do the experts in communication cease to examine the nature of what they are doing? Are the news-people in a TV production team too wrapped up in the process of meeting deadlines that they cannot spare time to reflect upon their role as mediators between the raw material of news and the way it is reconstructed for the TV screen? Practice, therefore, for communication studies students, serves a higher goal than expertise – namely, that of reflection. Each task is a means to better understanding, not an end in itself. It is a means of tackling problems, of identifying and analysing issues. By focusing on cases, on immediate and specific instances, the task-orientated approach seeks to cast a light on general truths.

In summary, then, the study of communication centres upon people as the makers, changers and interpreters of meaning. It is a subject which draws widely upon other fields of study for its evidence and for much of its theory. It is essentially a means of learning by doing, by discovery and by experiment.

Perhaps most importantly, it is a subject in which every step begins with a question: Who, What, Why, Where, When, How? Armed with these keywords the student steps forth into the most colourful and intriguing of activities – human com-munication; and if there is time and inclination, into the communication of other living creatures too.

2

The cornerstones of Communication Studies

When people ask what communication studies is all about they are usually seeking a list of topic headings. This is the easy part. One can cite the following as major areas of subject-matter:

Intrapersonal and interpersonal communication
Communication in groups and organizations
The 'languages' of communication (including art, music, film)
The development of information technology
Mass communication

The problem comes when these titles begin to be interpreted from the point of view of learning experience. How are the subjects to be taught/learnt? In what order? With what inter-connections? In what depth? From what angle? With what goals in mind? How can such vast expanses of human endeavour be systematized, reduced to manageable proportions?

As in all subjects, the syllabus offers a primary framework within which teachers and students can operate. The problem with communication studies is that frameworks are often awkwardly restricting. For example, to create a unit of the syllabus dedicated wholly to intra/interpersonal communica-tion might initially be logical and helpful to the student. How-ever, to draw a line round person-to-person communicative behaviour is to risk excluding some important factors: the world beyond immediate interaction affects the interaction in all sorts of ways. What Person A says to Person B may be influenced by what A has read in the papers or seen on TV. To appreciate the nature of A's interaction with B we might well have to study the impact which the media has had on A's message and B's reception of it. Communication is indivisible. If it is to be broken up into small, manageable portions in order to facilitate closer study, this fact has to be borne constantly in mind. Now if A happens to be the editor of a newspaper and B the owner of that newspaper, their interaction constitutes interpersonal communication. Yet the significance for us of such an interaction lies in what it might tell us about issues which come under the heading of mass communication – issues such as editorial freedom, ownership and control.

How, then, do we narrow things down? Fig. 7 represents a simple curriculum model which suggests that the four major elements of the curriculum are interdependent. The content of the course will draw direction from aims. It will receive support and illumination from concepts and theory, while aims, content and theory will be reinforced through application. Chapter 4 deals with the application of knowledge through skills so here I will concentrate on aims, content, concepts and theory, rounding off with a section on issues which represent an effective way of narrowing down content.

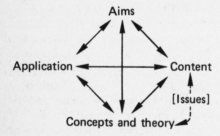

Fig. 7

Aims and priorities

As we have seen, communication studies represents a question-asking mode of approach to learning, so the following is a list of a few questions that students might ask at the beginning of a course, and then again during it and after it, to ensure that what they have been doing is meaningful:

What are the aims of study?
How do I go about achieving these aims?
Are the aims relevant?
What body of knowledge will be necessary to work towards

the attainment of aims?
What skills will I need?

The reader will correctly point out that such questions apply to practically every subject studied, that they are questions one should ask about one's education generally. We need to differentiate between course aims and student goals, for they are not necessarily one and the same. The goal of a communication student may be to get a job in the media. While a course in communication studies could add weight to a student's application for a media job, the aims of study are not so job-specific, otherwise we would be dealing with training rather than education.

I would suggest the following core aims for communication studies:

To encourage in the student a greater understanding of the nature and processes of communication.
To improve and diversify competence in communication.

In order to fulfil the above aims, students have to be convinced of their relevance, socially and personally. Social relevance may relate to the students' ambitions – to pass exams, to qualify for higher level courses or to get good jobs. Social relevance therefore affects motivation. If students consider that what they are doing is going to 'lead on to something', motivation is likely to be strong.

Yet relevance does not relate entirely to a system of external rewards such as exam passes and improved opportunities of employment. Personal relevance involves inner or intrinsic reward: a thing is worth doing for its own sake, because it is interesting, challenges the mind or stimulates creativity. 'I enjoyed doing that' is as important an indicator of relevance as the extrinsic statement 'Doing that helped me pass my exams'. True relevance comes about when there is a mix between extrinsic and intrinsic motivation and reward.

Let us be more specific about aims and quote here those of the Associated Examining Board (AEB) Communication Studies 'A' Level:

The aim of the syllabus is to promote knowledge of, understanding of, and competence in communication by:
1.1 study of categories, forms and uses of communication, in order

to interpret major theories and issues;
1.2 application of this study to *cases* drawn from authentic situations;
1.3 development of practical skills in communication.

These aims are expanded by the AEB into detailed objectives –
step-by-step approaches to the fulfilment of aims. For our
purposes here, we can distil the aims by picking out the key
words: *categories*, *forms*, *uses*, *theories*, *issues*, *cases*, *skills*.
The AEB lists categories as intrapersonal, interpersonal and
extrapersonal communication, group communication and
mass communication. Forms are classified as oral, written and
printed, non-verbal, graphical and numerical, and include new
technologies. Uses are divided into information processing,
persuasion, propaganda, publicity, entertainment, socialization and social functioning. Theory is classified under factors,
principles, hypotheses, findings, models and development.

The above subdivisions are not intended to be followed
slavishly, section by section, item by item. This would be to
misconstrue the spirit and intention of the curriculum. Rather
they should be seen as signposts to assist us in mapping jour-
neys where many paths cross and on a great many occasions
run parallel with one another. The signposts help us to look
out for things; they assist us in structuring our enquiries.
These, translated into questions about communication in a
large organization, might be:

To what *uses* is communication put?
What *forms* does that communication take?
How do such uses and forms relate to *theory*?
What research *findings* cast a light on our understanding of
communication in organizations?
What *issues* or matters of debate can we identify in looking
at communication within organizations?

The objective should be to use categorization as a means of
getting analysis or exploration under way, without categorization getting in the way of understanding. Also, we should be
ever-ready to re-focus our attention.

Application

When we know we have to do something with what we are
learning we pay special attention. Applying learning concen-

trates the faculties of eye, mind and hand. Tasks, for the most part, make us deal with specifics, what the AEB refers to as cases, for the cases are intended to offer us the nitty-gritty of real experience.

The authentic situation forms a base from which to develop hypotheses which further investigation, aligned perhaps with the findings of other researchers, might graduate into tentative theory.

There is the danger that application becomes an end in itself. A student could get so involved with the compelling detail of film making, for example, so absorbed with process, that everything but the task moves out of focus. This is obviously the time to stop, think, look back at the aims of communication studies and ask such questions as:

> Am I getting too involved in activity to consider the nature of the activity?
> How far has the experience of what I have been doing justified, or brought into question, my choice of medium?

It is advisable in any task to step back occasionally and take stock:

> Have I got my aims clear?
> Are these aims guiding the work I am doing?
> Am I clear about the reasons for the choice of my means of communication?
> Is what I am doing still appropriate for my envisaged audience?

Logs and diaries The AEB insists that A Level students preparing their Paper 3 (the Project) should write a detailed log or diary. Kept over several months, these student logs can be as significant as the finished product. Thoughtful logs, recording how students go about their project preparation and its progress, are places of reflection on the process of communication itself.

In Fig. 8 (overleaf), thinking about the difficulty of gleaning information from strangers, our student has come up with a principle which is hard to refute, and one which all students doing research beyond the confines of libraries should take to heart. Once recognized, that principle can save time, aid decision-making and produce results.

October 5th

So many closed doors. I've written more than
20 letters to the companies I need to get
information from. It's because I'm a
stranger, writing out of the blue. They're
too busy. Yet today was a breakthrough. My
Uncle John had given me a name to phone. It
made all the difference - that is, having a
contact. One little word from my uncle, and
Mr Grey couldn't have been more helpful.

Must remember, one personal contact is worth
a hundred letters between strangers. But how
to make more contacts? Perhaps I ought to
pretend I'm a big movie producer from Hollywood
- that might make them sit up and take notice.

Fig. 8

Fig. 9 shows another example of a log entry in which experience is being translated into learning. What our student is discovering through experience and reflection is a concept which holds good not merely for one instance but for many. Any communication studies student will soon be able to recognize the role of the 'gate keeper'. In all walks of life, especially in hierarchies, official or unofficial gate keepers are to be found, holding the gate open to some, keeping it firmly shut to others.

November 18th

Every time I ring up this advertising manager,
I'm sort of blocked by his secretary. Either
he's busy on another line or he's in a
meeting. She won't say when he's going to
be free. Just keep on ringing, she says.
I reckon she's protecting him from the likes
of me.

Fig. 9

A log then, helps experience and observation germinate into ideas. A scrapbook of cuttings from newspapers and periodicals will also provide a good source of information too recent to be found in books.

Theory

In constructing theory we try to give ideas some shape; we seek to connect up ideas, to make distinctive patterns out of them; we use ideas, based on experience and learning, to make sense of things. This is called *cognition* or thinking. Theory may be defined as 'a way of explaining something'. Where theory sets out to explain the behaviour of people it can obviously never aspire to the exactness of a scientific theory: it works towards a greater truth without ever becoming an incontrovertible law. Theory is not something to be frightened of. It should be welcomed as a short-cut to understanding. Take, for example, two minor and competing theories which communication studies students are likely to encounter – those of *primacy* and *recency*. The first states that what a person or an audience sees or hears first sticks longest; has most impact. The second asserts the reverse, that what counts most is what is seen or heard last.

Stimulus for enquiry   What we have here is the base-line for thought and investigation – a framework for question-asking. Most of us will probably acknowledge from our own experience that 'first impressions die hard', so we might give initial credence to the theory of primacy. We would examine the case for primacy by considering ways in which the theory may be demonstrated – first impressions of people; the first speech in a debate; the political party which gets in first with its election manifesto or takes a head start with its campaign strategy. Our theory has launched us into discussion and enquiry. We seek to test the theory to destruction or till it holds up. In the process of testing, we try out alternative explanations, tease out those factors other than timing which make messages 'stick'.

Theorizing is not only for teachers, researchers or philosophers. You can do it, and you start by getting a picture in your head, an idea. Let us imagine that you went to a big party last night. You are lying in the bath, thinking about it. Intuitively, it might occur to you that in all the conversations you were involved in and in all the conversations you saw going on, it seemed to be the males of the species who did most of the talking. Your observations might set up a connection in your brain: you remember in a recent class discussion someone protested that the men did not allow the women a word in edgeways. The connection poses a question: in mixed company, do men dominate the discourse? A *hypothesis* has been born. It is obviously a long way from becoming a theory, but it is something to work on. What will you need to do to move hypothesis towards theory? You obviously need more evidence and that evidence must be rigorous. It must anticipate counterarguments.

Avoiding dogmatism   In the process of research, you may encounter lots of people who go round with their heads bursting with 'theories': 'Of course women talk less,' one pundit might declare, 'it's because women have less to say.' We have not got a theory here but a *stereotype* based on ignorance connected with prejudice rather than observation linked with an open mind.

Another person you might discuss the hypothesis with could proffer a more constructive explanation: 'Yes, women talk less in mixed company, but that's because of their socialization.'

Plainly this person has gone beyond the surface facts – that in certain situations women talk less in public than men – and has asked *why* this might be so.

Even if exhaustively-summoned evidence pushes hypothesis towards theory, we are still only at the beginning of our pursuit of understanding. We do not create theories in order to be ruled by them. Having asked why socialization may have influenced women into being less talkative in mixed company; having examined the factors in that socialization which might have contributed to the hypothesis, we need to ask a further question: how can the situation be changed? We do not resign ourselves to our findings if we are maturing through the relativist stage of intellectual and emotional development. We are committed to action, to bettering conditions which do not appear to us to be fair, honest or equitable.

Encountering hunch theory   Because communication is an integral part of everything we do in life, it has been fertile ground for theories. Many of these are little more than hunches – guessology – but that does not prevent them being influential and being acted upon.

Theorizing occurs wherever there are *issues*, wherever there are problems. If there appears to be an increase in violence in society, there will be no shortage of those attempting to establish connections between this violence and that which appears on the cinema or TV screen. The media themselves latch on to this 'theory'; any evidence that appears to support such theory is used in support. It is often oversimplified in the process. What begins as a hunch may become a self-fulfilling prophecy: the headlines dramatize and amplify; there are calls in public for 'something to be done'. An issue, by means of hunch theory based upon (usually) slender evidence, has become a crisis:

Event + Publicity + Theorizing = Issue
Issue + Publicity + Theorizing = Crisis

It is all too easy to be carried away by theory; to have things apparently 'settled' by it. In fact, it is extremely difficult to prove a connection between screen violence and real violence. The connection may exist. Common sense tells us that television does influence audiences in many ways so that it may also influence an audience's response to violence.

Communication studies students must, however, remain ever on guard, cautious in accepting sweeping explanations of things. Further, students should probe beyond the theory to the attitudes behind it, the motives of those who give credence, and amplification, to the argument.

From the beginning of our examination of theory we have to be clear about one of its central and unavoidable ingredients, *ideology*. By this we mean our beliefs in the way things are and should be. Ideology is so much a part of us that very often we do not recognize its influence upon us (I refer to ideology in a little more detail in Chapter 3). Ideology colours our judgement and shapes our perceptions – about audience, for example. If we have a very low opinion of people's intelligence and independence of mind, we might subscribe to the so-called hypodermic needle theory of mass communication. The notion here is that the mass media 'inject' their messages into a largely passive and accepting audience. The implications, therefore, are serious: the mass media are deemed to have immense power to influence and manipulate the attitudes and opinions of the audience, which also constitutes an electorate.

For newspaper barons, this theory may be worth supporting because it helps justify heavy investment; it indicates power. In this case, theory and vested interest form a happy union, ideologically compatible.

Communication studies students will come into contact with a spectrum of attitudes towards other people, towards audience, which colours both theory and behaviour, as in Fig. 10.

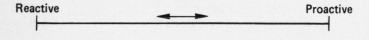

Fig. 10

The view represented at the left hand of the scale is that people simply react to stimuli. They tend to believe what they are told, accepting uncritically the information and explanations provided them. At the proactive end of the scale, people are seen as doing something with the information, attitudes and ideas by which they are stimulated. That is, they contribute their own information, attitudes and ideas to the message provided. They change what they receive; they may even reject it.

Theories of mass communication find themselves somewhere along the scale, which students may discover to be a useful rule of thumb in examining theory and investigating audience response. We immediately realize that as individuals we respond differently along the scale to different information. For instance, if we know something about a topic being dealt with in the press or on TV we may respond very proactively; if we know nothing about the subject, or care nothing for it, our response might be located towards the reactive end of the scale. It would be misleading as well as unfair to classify us as reactive persons because of this; once again, stereotyping has taken place.

Stereotyping is the first step in dehumanizing people. Therefore it is dangerous. The hypodermic theory perceives people as being substantially automatons. Like most hunch theories, it takes a reactive view of humanity, oversimplifying the complexity of human responses and of the many influences upon us other than those exerted by the mass media.

A reference to principles We are at the point where a focus upon theory requires a further focus – on principles of communication practice, or *postulates*, one of which is that communication is proactive (Mortensen 1972, see Appendix A). People are not empty receptacles to be filled with information, ideas, beliefs, attitudes and values. Proving proactivity rather than reactivity is one justification for studying human communication. The basic postulate that communication occurs whenever people attribute significance to message-related behaviour can be divided into five secondary postulates:

1 Communication is dynamic (in a constant process of movement and change).
2 Communication is irreversible (once a thing has been said it can never be unsaid).
3 Communication is proactive.
4 Communication is interactive.
5 Communication is contextual (is influenced by and influences its environment).

With such postulates, principles or precepts in mind, we may avoid the trap of oversimplification and will have the confidence to reject hunch theories, or at least will subject them to careful scrutiny.

Issues

Issues can be defined as 'Those social, cultural, economic or political concerns or ideas which are, at any given time, considered important, and which are the source of debate, controversy, or conflict' (see Watson and Hill, Appendix A). Issues concentrate attention; they constitute problems which have to be investigated, and because they are current there is usually plenty of information about them – or at least plenty of comment. We need to discriminate between issues in general and communication issues which chiefly centre around the control of information and expression, the nature of that control and the reasons for it. We remain interested, of course, in the ways in which the media deal with major issues of the time – such as law and order, industrial unrest, nuclear disarmament; and these ways often constitute communication issues, of bias, stereotyping, misinformation and censorship.

In examining communication issues, we are generally perceiving information as a source of power and influence, not only that wielded by the media but that by government and those in positions of authority – with access to and control over information – at all levels of society.

Of the great human freedoms, those of speech and expression and of access to information concern us especially in communication studies. What information is kept on us? How is it to be used? Do we have a right to check that information for accuracy? Who has access to that information?

Similarly, as a community and a nation, how much information which is important to us as citizens is being withheld from us, and why? Indeed how much information about us is being gathered without our knowing? Have we, as citizens, a right to know about the processes of surveillance which the new technology of computers has made possible?

An issue of very long standing is that of the ownership and control of the mass media, particularly that of the press. The ownership of the national and regional press has fallen into fewer and fewer hands. Increasingly newspapers have been bought up by multi-national corporations: the printed word becomes just another commodity along with oil products, motorway cafes or diamond mines. What are the issues here? What happens if a newspaper belonging to a multi-national corporation attacks the labour relations of one of that corporation's subsidiary companies?

Interference   One irrefutable truth is that the free flow of information is eternally subject to interference, either before that information has been communicated, or after it. The interference comes about because of the fear, on the part of the 'interferer', of the effects the communication of information may have – on the electorate, on business interests, on foreign 'enemies', on the young and vulnerable, on circulation figures or audience rating; and this is where clashes or conflicts of interest or viewpoint occur.

Below are a few effects-type questions covering some of the major communication issues of our time:

How far does the portrayal of violence in the media influ-

ence the attitudes of audience to violence in 'real life';
can the portrayal of violence create 'copy-cat' behaviour?
To what extent does the presence of TV cameras/reporters
act as a catalyst to violence in situations of conflict?
How persuasive are the media?
What impact on society, and upon the media themselves,
will the advancing technology of video, cable and satellite
transmission have?
What cultural effects is Western information/media technology – hardware and software – having upon developing
Third World nations?
What effect is the growth of sophisticated information stor-
age and retrieval systems going to have on: government,
business and industry, international relations, education,
personal privacy?

Such issues, once they have been discussed and analysed,
prompt us into examining available research findings, and
probably conducting modest research tasks ourselves. It is also
an appropriate time for looking at the various modes of analysis and research as well as finding out about research bodies
and the work of research teams. The reports of the many royal
commissions and committees of enquiry into the press and
broadcasting form rich quarries of information and ideas.

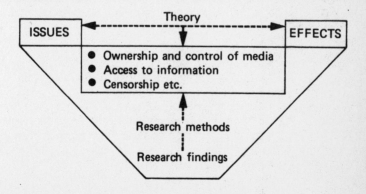

Fig. 11

In this chapter I have stressed the need to structure our learning in order to render this vast field of study 'graspable'. To do this, we need to keep constantly in mind the inter-relationship between clear aims, relevant content and appropriate application. We have seen that the establishment of principles and the potential of theory help us to link up areas of knowledge and experience, and direct and reinforce our learning. We have seen that issues provide a further focus in our selection of relevant content. Constantly at our elbow, we should keep a checklist of questions to glance at now and then to make sure we have not got lost in the communication forest without a compass:

Is what I am doing still in line with course aims?

Is there a danger of doubling back on myself, going over old ground rather than progressing to new learning?

In applying myself to specific tasks, am I thinking about the nature of what I am doing?

How much of what I have learnt have I accepted without questioning?

How proactive have I been as opposed to being reactive?

3

The language of Communication Studies

'I've just looked up a dictionary,' a student of mine announced one day, 'and there's no such word as "encoder".' 'It's probably under "code",' I replied. But the question behind the query remained: 'Why do we have to learn so many extra words? So much jargon?'

Communication studies does have some generally unfamiliar and occasionally formidable terminology, like any other academic subject. In *What is Linguistics?*, another book in this series, David Crystal says that 'In fact, jargon – if all one means by this is 'technical terms' – is an essential part of the apparatus of any intellectual discipline'. Just as a student of botany must be able to name plants and the individual parts of those plants (rather than saying, 'that little blue flower with the top bit in the shape of a bell'), so communication studies students must have names for things, for quick identification and in order to work at levels beyond common knowledge.

This overview of the subject is not the place for an exhausting hike around the terminology of interpersonal and mass communication. This would be as confusing as attempting to see all the paintings in the National Gallery in half an hour. Here, then, is a selection of some of the most significant and useful items.

First, it is important to familiarize ourselves with the nature of a *discourse*. The simple dictionary definition of this word is, 'talk, converse; hold forth in speech and writing on a subject'. When we refer to a learned discourse we are acknowledging that the talk, conversation or holding forth is pitched at a certain level of understanding; a level that assumes a degree of learning and knowledge, and a recognition of the significance of that learning and knowledge.

Tuning in to discourse

Communication studies is itself a discourse: it uses language, information, ideas, concepts and theories for which a degree of 'tuning in' is necessary if participation is to be seen to be purposeful. Communication studies is also a study *of* discourses – identifying them, analysing them, comparing and contrasting them.

You will learn to discriminate not only between the many kinds of discourse but between those which are dominant and those which are subordinate. You will be encouraged to examine the links between dominant social or cultural groups and dominant discourses, see Fig. 12.

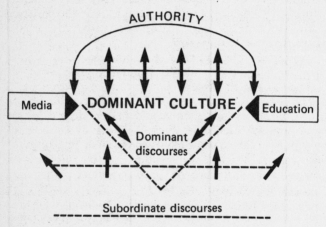

Fig. 12

Written or spoken language is obviously central to the discourse, but its nature (its level and complexity) is decided by the rules of discourse which themselves are shaped by the goals and values of those who 'dominate' the discourse. Thus in schools, the dominant discourse of the classroom is shaped and controlled by the teachers who are themselves 'in tune' (if they want their pupils to succeed) with the wider educational expectations of the community. Of course there are plenty of subordinate discourses in school as anywhere else in society. One of these is the 'language of the playground', a discourse between pupils to which teachers rarely have access. Pupils create sub-cultures which deviate from the dominant culture of the school; using the various codes or languages of their sub-cultures, they make and sustain friendship. However, as things are, if they wish to 'succeed in the world', they must also be able to work in the codes set for them by the dominant culture.

In the mass media, there are many discourses – overlapping, intermingling, often competing against one another. Let us take TV news as an example of a discourse which receives special attention because it 'sounds forth' to mass audiences. One of the rules of this discourse is to be informative, to present the facts 'as they are'. One might term that a *news value*. Yet to be informative is only one of the major declared functions of television. Without risking too much contradiction, we could describe *entertainment* as being the dominant function of most television, with perhaps education still in the running, but a long way behind. Consequently there is pressure for information to be presented 'entertainingly'. Too many 'talking heads' on the news – or indeed any programme – will, it is considered, bore the viewer. Additionally, there are pressures which arise from the nature of the medium itself. A visual medium requires pictures, the more dramatic, the better. That constitutes another news value.

The facts in our news discourse are not only being presented 'as they are', but how television likes to present them: entertainingly and visually. The question immediately arises – what if the news item is not easily communicated in visual terms? Might it lose place in a news bulletin to an item which comes with 'good pictures'? Might it fail even to get on to the news editors' agenda?

Agenda-setting

The term *agenda-setting* is a crucial one to our studies. An agenda is the list of matters to be discussed and decided upon in a meeting. Whether it is a clay-pigeon shooting club, the directorial board of a multi-national company or a cabinet meeting, there are rules to be followed to ensure efficiency, order and fair-play. If you are a member of a students' union committee you know that, however important an issue is to you, it is no good leaping up and attempting to overrule procedures.

Although there are ways in which urgent, last-minute business can be dealt with in a meeting in advance of other agenda items, if those who draw up the agenda refuse to alter it, you will usually have to win a substantial 'vote from the floor' to get your way. Agenda-setting, then, is about listing items of priority; about selection and about ways of doing things. It is also about ways of thinking and perceiving.

TV news reflects the ways of perceiving, thinking and valuing of the practitioners of television craft. They are, as it were, 'go-betweens', in a position to 'mediate' between the events of the world as they happen and the news as it is presented in sound and image. They, and those who employ them, shape the discourse of news, and the themes making up this news discourse will be edited and angled according to news values.

If action, especially violent action, constitutes a value, then news discourse could find more of interest in *effects* rather than causes; in violence on picket lines rather than the causes of the picketing. What might be read as a story about unemployment and the struggle for jobs could be re-told as a story about law and order: the original theme of unemployment may become subordinate to the dominant theme of law and order.

The concept of mediation

The analysis of the notions and practice of mediation is central to the interpretation of communication processes at all levels. We are all mediators: using the means of communication, we re-construct reality as we perceive it – though not always consciously.

Recently I received a message from an acquaintance who had bought a book I had written. The message, via my wife, was that the book had made 'good lavatory reading'. This I took as a compliment. I got the intended meaning of the message because of several contextual factors, one of them simply defined by punctuation.

The phrase 'lavatory reading' could be used in two ways. The use of quotation marks – that's how I read the message even though it was spoken and passed on by word of mouth –

indicated that the phrase was lightly or ironically meant. It also had a literal meaning in that the book had very likely been read, at some time or another, in the lavatory – hence the ironic use of the phrase.

I am aware, and so was the sender of the message, as well as my wife as mediator, that lavatory reading could be deemed an insulting way of describing a book and its contents. How then could I be so certain of the *preferred reading* of my acquaintance's message? Very largely, in this case, because of the *tone* in which the message was reported by a messenger I trusted. If my wife had, on the other hand, received a message saying that my book was 'little better than lavatory reading', her role as mediator could well have been more pronounced. Out of consideration for me she might have laundered the message to make it acceptable to me; or – the privilege of the mediator – she might have censored our acquaintance's comment altogether.

Every time we report an incident we have witnessed or a conversation we have heard, we are mediating between reality as it exists and reality as we perceive it. We know very well the unreliability of witnesses to accidents: one might say ten witnesses, ten accidents.

What factors contribute to people perceiving things differently? This question is a tantalizing one to be born constantly in mind. Much of our perception process is taken up with selecting in and selecting out; we are editors of what we experience. For one thing, we pay attention to matters which are important to us. These, we can recall and report. If we disapprove of what we have seen or heard we may modify – or select – the facts to be reported; and the language in which we choose to report the facts will be adjusted. Much depends on who we are (what our *self-concept* is), what our personal values are, who our audience is and the context of the communication.

When the media communicate messages, they are similarly influenced. The difference is that the processes of mediation, from reality to presentation, are considerably more complicated because there are so many stages through which information has to pass on its way to the front page of a newspaper or the opening headlines of the TV news, as in Fig. 13.

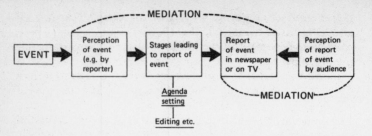

Fig. 13

The construction of reality   One of the most misleading 'truths' is that the camera never lies. In fact, the camera is an inveterate liar; and the photographic image can be manipulated more easily even than statistics. Every time a camera is pointed in one direction rather than another, every time hard focus is selected rather than soft focus, every time a close-up is preferred to a long-shot, mediation is taking place. From the moment a news photographer and reporter are sent out to cover one story rather than another, reality – the 'great out-there' – is being reconstructed, interpreted, translated into a news discourse heavily flavoured with 'media salt' (that is, entertainment). The picture of reality is cropped, scissored to size for the paper, or edited down to fit the TV news slot. The captions or the commentary further frame the shot. What goes before it on the news agenda, and what follows it, impinge on the way the message is conveyed and received.

Performance   What I have written above constitutes back-stage comment, intended to delve behind what has been termed the *front region* (Goffman 1971, see Appendix A), the on-stage performance. Professional communicators in the media are not going to come out and announce openly on their front pages or on TV that audiences should beware of mediation.

Like good professionals (indeed like magicians) they are not going to divulge back-stage secrets. That would flavour the performance with cynicism. The aim at all times is to give the impression that news is presented 'as it is and as it happens', that the agenda of news items is practically self-selecting: major headlines, major stories come before minor ones in a natural order.

This attitude among media professionals amounts to a

belief, often sincerely held, but one requiring close examination. For such an examination to take place, it is vital to grasp the concept of *ideology* and the role it plays at every level of communication, especially in mass communication.

The role of ideology

Ideology can be defined as a collection of ideas about what ought to be in a community or a nation. If the press is to be believed, the world is split between two competing ideologies – the capitalism of the West and the communism of the East. It is part of ideology to perceive these rivals as essentially opposites, and irreconcileable, whether this is true or not, believing it helps to sustain and support the power struggle, to maintain the clear definition of 'them' and 'us'.

That, by and large, is the message of the dominant ideology emanating from those dominant sectors of society which have access to, and often control over, the means of mass communication. Yet ideology ought not to be seen as something imposed necessarily from above: top people telling us what to believe and what to think. Rather, ideology is present in all acts of communication. It is so much with us, so much a part of us that we do not always recognize it. Often we have so thoroughly taken ideology on board – internalized it – that it appears as natural as the air we breath. John Mepham's revealing and significant comment that we are not blinded by ideology but blind *to* it could explain the anger media people feel when accused of allowing ideology to suffuse their news pages or broadcasts. They are often honestly unaware that, despite their aspirations to objectivity, ideology is working in them and through them, see Fig. 14.

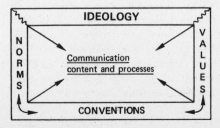

Fig. 14

One of the outward and visible signs of ideology – and one of its prime agents – is the *metaphor*, defined as a figure of speech 'by which a thing is spoken of as being that which it only resembles', according to my dictionary. In newspaper headlines, the metaphor has the initial power of concentrating and dramatizing:

WORLD FINANCIAL STORM KNOCKS GOVERN-MENT POLICY OFF COURSE.

Where certain dominant values and interests are under threat, metaphor becomes a weapon to stir up heightened emotional responses – to unfurl the banner of ideological differences:

PRIME MINISTER DECLARES WAR ON UNIONS

The favourite metaphor of the media is the military metaphor. Where ideologies clash, metaphor – military metaphor – reigns: thus a factory is 'besieged' by protesting workers; strikers 'threaten to hold the nation to ransom', 'armies' of soccer fans 'storm' the terraces. We are, as readership or audience, invited to take sides in the ideological confrontation, to approve or disapprove, to give support and reinforcement. In short, to accept the *consensus* view of things.

Consensus: who is qualified to define it?   Consensus means 'what the majority of us agree on'. Upon what evidence do the press and TV represent and articulate consensus? In order to speak for the so-called 'silent majority', which the press in particular claim to do, they must surely have detailed access to the opinions of each and every one of us. This is patently impossible. In other words, they are qualified to speak only because they are equipped to speak, to many millions. Their control of the means of mass communication enables them to contribute substantially to dominant discourses; to set agendas about what information ought to be handled, in what ways and in what order. Consensus in this context is not what we agree upon, but what we are said to agree upon.

By the same token, the mass media are in a position to define the situation; by defining what is consensus they are also arbiters of what is *dissensus*, what is deviant. At the point where deviance is perceived to be a threat, the role of the media becomes *crisis definition*, alerting the community to developments that might imperil consensus, arguably another term for the status quo, the 'way things are'. In this sense, crisis not only threatens society, it shapes it, because by defining crisis the media almost inevitably – by focusing national attention upon it – amplify it (commentators call this an *amplification spiral*). If the discourse of the moment is concerned with a 'law and order crisis' in society, then action is called for, usually in the form of laws to render 'deviance' more difficult. At the same time, dissent from 'consensus' is at risk.

The search for meaning

Perhaps the most important term in all communication studies (and in the humanities generally) is *meaning*. Some commentators would have it that people communicate primarily to fulfil needs, and it is certainly true that we employ communication for a wide range of functions: instrumental ('Please pass the salt'); control ('Don't do that, it's dangerous'); information ('Is this the way to Nether Wallop?'); expression (in writing, song, dance etc.); social (the company of others); affiliation (love, affection); the alleviation of anxiety (telling somebody about your problems); stimulation (of curiosity, one's sense of adventure); and role-related (what one's role at any particular time demands).

The psychologist and educationalist Abraham Maslow has argued that needs form a hierarchy, starting with basic survival needs (such as eating, sleeping, drinking, obtaining shelter) and working upwards towards what he calls *self-actualization*, see Fig. 15.

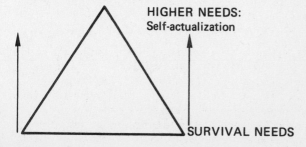

HIGHER NEEDS:
Self-actualization

SURVIVAL NEEDS

Fig. 15

For Maslow, the realization of self is the human being's highest, most meaningful aspiration. Communication plays a central part in the process whereby people discover and develop the best in themselves. Foremost among the characteristics which mark self-actualization is independence. Critics of Maslow's view believe that he leaves off too soon. Independence, yes. That is what most good education sets out to achieve in students – but independence for *what*? Victor Frankl talks of a further goal – the *will to meaning*, shown in the pursuit of important values to do with creativity, experience and attitudes. In brief, humans aspire to be transcendent of self, to discover freedom by relating beyond self to others, to the outside world, see Fig. 16.

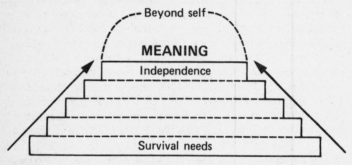

Fig. 16

Unless, in our studies, we can keep that wide framework in mind, we may perceive communication too narrowly, and use it too narrowly. However, having set our sights ambitiously, we must acknowledge that meaning is not unlike the way beauty is often defined – something that exists in the eye of the beholder, which is debatable and open to influence.

Assigning meaning   Two people may be looking at a painting. One says, 'It doesn't mean anything to me'. The other might reply, 'I see a lot of meaning in it'. How do we attempt to find out who's right about the painting? What would we need to know before we could hazard a judgement?

It would be very convenient if the answer were simply to ask the artist; after all, he or she ought to know. But does meaning actually belong with, or to, the artist; or does meaning extend to the viewers of the picture? And if that is the case, is one person's view of the meaning of the picture as good as anybody else's?

Semiology, the scientific study of signs, offers us a useful key to the exploration of meaning. Essentially, the semiologist believes that meaning is not delivered, like a package from sender to receiver but it is *assigned*. We, as audience, give meaning *to* things. If this is the case, then the 'receiving end' of the communication process is given far more emphasis than it has been in traditional – linear – models and theory.

Person A no longer simply conveys message X to person B, complete with built-in meaning. Only at the point where negotiation begins, between person A and person B, does meaning begin. In other words, meaning begins with person B. The role of the receiver or decoder is suddenly of vital significance: the audience ceases to be a passive receptacle, but is a proactive, on-stage performer in the negotiation of meaning.

When we look at the hypothetical painting mentioned above, and remember that its meaning is something 'up for negotiation', we experience a change in attitude towards it. Originally we may have considered meaning as something locked into the picture, part of the artist's secret. We feel ourselves excluded, even alienated: 'I don't understand it – it's rubbish!' Yet if meaning is something attributed to a text as well as merely emanating from it (or not emanating), our own contribution is all at once important. Instead of a one-way line of address, communication has become an *interaction*, as in Fig. 17.

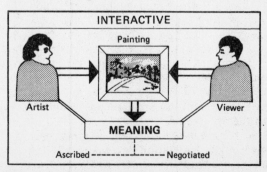

Fig. 17

Unpacking the text   The pursuit of meaning may be said to advance through two levels or orders of perception: the denotative level and the connotative level of meaning. With *denotation* we are at the descriptive level of analysis. A newspaper picture of an aircraft carrier leaving harbour denotes the basic information that a ship is on its way to manoeuvres or to war. However, the picture – at a deeper level – may connote valour, patriotism or power. It serves as a metaphor for these qualities: the warship symbolizes the ship of state. It is at the level of *connotation* that we encounter meaning, or *signification*.

Similarly, we attempt to probe the 'text' of interpersonal relationships in search of their deeper connotation. Person A, standing close to Person B, might denote the fact that they are involved in a task which requires them to stand next to each other; it might also connote the fact that, by narrowing the space between them, Person A and Person B are signifying that they are in love.

In 'reading the text' of Person A and Person B we would have to observe those signs which are indicators of meaning – their body language, their *non-verbal communication* – as well as what they say to one another. We would be interested in the way their eyes meet, their facial expressions, their gestures (*kinesics*) and the incidence of touch. We would find ourselves involved in *proxemics*, the analysis of the way people manage space between themselves and others.

If Person A and Person B decide they do not want the world to know about their love affair, they will confine love-behaviour to the back region of their human 'performance'. Their front region performance will denote discretion. They will keep a social rather than an intimate distance between them when they are in public. We, as observers suspecting the 'real' relationship between them – connoting this relationship – will be on the look out for role strain, for clues to the tension felt by each partner under the constraint of having to 'behave in public', to keep the back region performance separate from that of the front region.

Plainly there is likely to be more consensus about levels of denotation than those of connotation. With denotation, little more is required than to read the text, 'A and B are friends'; with connotation, we have to read *in* to the text, 'A and B are pretending to be just friends, but . . .'. The connotative level or order is what signifies – where meaning resides, and at all times in our dealings with texts we should be pushing beyond the level of denotation to that of connotation.

Taking a case

In order to recap some of the terms I have introduced in this chapter, let us examine a well-known painting such as *The Yellow Chair* by Vincent Van Gogh. You will find the original of this painting housed in The National Gallery, in London, and it is reproduced in several good art history books, including *Van Gogh* by W. Udhe (Oxford: Phaidon, 1981). We will have no difficulty agreeing that it denotes a chair, with pipe and tobacco pouch, in an empty room. At the denotative level we might describe the text of the painting as a reproduction in oils of a favourite chair which had served the artist well. If we look at the painting from the point of view of Van Gogh, we can categorize it as an example of intrapersonal communication. The artist is addressing himself through paint, investigating his personal response to the exterior objects which are of special significance to him.

He has chosen to work with a particular set of signs, marks on canvas, within a code – a coherent arrangement of these signs – in a particular medium, through the channel of hand and eye. At the same time we can be confident that Van Gogh's intention is not confined to encoding a message purely for his own consumption. He is communicating something to us, his audience. The painting is, then, also an act of interpersonal communication.

If we switch attention from the artist to the perceived audience, the possibilities for 'reading the signs' multiply. Van Gogh's original audience might have been his beloved brother Theo who supported Vincent financially throughout his life. The message of the painting, its *preferred reading* might have been clear and explicit to Theo and to Vincent's painter friends. It was probably far less clear to the general public of the time. Many were put off by Van Gogh's 'crude' use of his medium, and we know the artist sold few pictures during his lifetime.

Changing perceptions Yet today audiences are far more
receptive to the art of Van Gogh. He is admired, cherished and
even loved. So popular has Van Gogh become that his work is
reproduced in many different printed forms. What began as a
unique event, has, through mass production, become univer-
sally available. Technology has mediated between the original
work and its new audience. It has altered the context in which
the works of Van Gogh can be seen – from the art gallery to
the home, school, hospital, dentist's waiting room or execu-
tive washroom. Even its medium has altered, from the rough-
textured oil painting to the glossy print, poster, postcard or
calendar; and its dimensions have been varied to fit differing
requirements.

So, while the pictorial image does not change, our reading
of that image is subject to constant change – over time,
between different people, in different contexts. We all of us
bring to a text our own ways of seeing and interpreting, so the
important focus becomes the interaction between the work
and the audience.

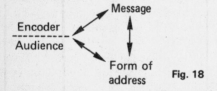

Fig. 18

In Fig. 18 a dynamic relationship is established between the
elements of the communication process, as the two-way
arrows suggest. If the reader feels the diagram is somehow
incomplete, he or she is welcome to add to it or rearrange it.

There is obviously more to Van Gogh's picture than the mere
replication of a chair, pipe and tobacco pouch. What the artist
perceived was a structure within a context. He was interested
in aspects of shape, form, texture, colour and perspective. We
might describe these as comprising an *aesthetic discourse*.

Deeper meaning At the connotative level it is the emptiness
of the chair which signifies most tellingly; and the emptiness
may connote the augury of approaching death, of the artist's
absence from the scene. We have a clue to this signification
because in 1883 Van Gogh told his brother a story he had read

about Charles Dickens and the illustrator Luke Fildes whose drawing of Dickens' own chair appeared in a periodical shortly after the novelist's death. Van Gogh possessed an engraving of the drawing. For the artist, then, the empty chair symbolized a loss through death.

Readers may already have noted that I am mediating between them and *The Yellow Chair*, highlighting those aspects that capture my attention, ignoring, perhaps, others. I may very well be guilty, in reading the text of the Van Gogh, of *aberrantly decoding* its message, just as I might, intentionally or unintentionally, misread the preferred meaning of a TV news broadcast.

I can only substantiate my analysis by paying a great deal of attention to each text under scrutiny: thinking about it, asking questions about it, comparing it to similar and contrasting texts, reading up what the experts say, testing out the texts for audience response; in short, studying, with the precept always in mind that study is the pursuit of meaning.

Ultimately, it has to be remembered that meaning lies in people and that it is negotiated: truth is at best an approximation, not an absolute.

In this chapter I have identified and tried to explain briefly only the most vital terms used in studying communication. In line with good study skills practice, put the book aside for a moment and try to recall what has been said about the following terms, as if describing them to another person:

Discourse
    Dominant
    Subordinate
Agenda-Setting
Mediation
Ideology
Consensus
Meaning/Signification
    Denotation
    Connotation

What other terms can you recall which have been omitted from the list? Finally, by glancing again at your painting of Van Gogh, how many terms can you make use of in analysing *The Yellow Chair*?

4

Acquiring and using the skills of Communication Studies

The first thing students usually ask is: What will I actually be *doing* in communication studies? Other questions might be: What sort of written work is involved? Will my ability to cope with the spoken word be assessed? Will there be opportunities for film making? What will I be doing that a future employer might find of value? The answers to such questions will depend on the nature of the communication course, the ideas of the teacher, the amount of time and equipment available and the competence and motivation of others in the group. However, there are areas of common agreement about what might be expected of the student.

First, a disclaimer: communication studies is *not* English by another name; nor is it what has been called 'business English', with skills activities directed exclusively toward the world of work. In English, business or otherwise, the word rules, while in communication studies the written or printed word is considered as only one of many different forms of communication; a sign system among important rivals.

This is not to argue that such standard English and business English skills as summarizing, comprehending verbal and graphic data, writing essays and reports or composing letters are irrelevant for communication studies students. In fact students may find themselves regularly involved in applying all these skills, yet for individual purposes rather than as routine class exercises.

Skills as means towards ends

For example, in any 'doing' course of study, students will expect to complete assignments which involve research not only among books and other material sources, but among people. If students have projects to do, they may have to write letters. Such letters are acts of communication and ambassadors at the same time. A well-expressed letter, making its points simply and accurately is likely to win a positive response. A badly written, confused letter will put off the receiver and no help may arrive.

Students may find that they are asked to meet people personally, to draw out from others the most relevant information in an interview situation. That requires practice in order to build up confidence and competence. In communication studies, being able to conduct an interview is as important as being able to perform well in a job interview. The one is useful practice for the other.

There are five areas of skills competence which are central to communication studies (as well as many other subjects):

Information seeking and recording
Analysing and evaluating
Responding
Applying knowledge
Creating

Few skills or competencies are discrete, that is, entirely separate from others; and some competencies, like interviewing, are made up of several skills, so we must bear that in mind as we examine each of the above divisions.

Information seeking and recording

Most students develop skill in matters such as memory, concentration, use of the library and other sources of information such as slides, audiotapes and data on overhead projection transparencies. That is a good beginning, but only a beginning.

The attentive ear   A skill rarely mentioned in textbooks is listening. Every student of communication must become an attentive listener – not only to the teacher in class but to all communicative sounds around him or her. The air buzzes with messages: on the bus, in the train, over the bar in the local pub; and very often it crackles with *noise*. There are two main categories of noise to be aware of – *engineering* noise, or technical noise, where there is physical interference with the message, and *semantic* noise, where the meaning of the message is somehow impeded. People are said to be 'talking at cross purposes', 'not being on the same wavelength', or 'not talking the same language'. These are semantic differences and they are the stuff of communication studies analysis.

Listening is crucial in all sorts of communicative ways: in discussion and debate, in interviewing, in 'reading' the situation between people during interpersonal communication, in investigating the nature of group activity and indeed in scrutinizing the conflicts and misunderstandings which arise between nations. The phrase, 'the dialogue of the deaf' resounds through international relations, indicating the prevalence of *selective listening*, that is, countries listening only to what they want to hear – a characteristic, of course, of individuals as well as nations.

In his article 'Barriers and Gateways to Communication', the American F.J. Roethlisberger[1] writes: 'The biggest block to personal communication is man's inability to listen intelligently, understandingly, and skillfully to another person.' It is a truism but well worth repeating, as is his conclusion that 'this deficiency in the modern world is widespread and appalling'.

The probing eye   If a prime duty of communication students is to listen, another is to observe. Looking is one of the great doing words of communication studies. Let us put it another way: the task of the student is to keep an eye on the *signs* – a questioning eye. Wherever we look we are bombarded with signs: words, pictures, images, and combinations of words and images. We look at an advertisement in a magazine, on a billboard or on television. We recognize that the combination of signs is intended to persuade us, on the surface, to buy a product or a service; beyond the surface, we may suspect, is a deeper motive – to lure us into 'buying' images, values, and even dreams.

All the while, communication studies students are exerting their powers of observation, of visual discrimination within the framework of those questions suggested at the end of Chapter 1: Who, What, Why, Where, When and How? As long

[1] Published in *Harvard Business Review* 30, July–August 1952.

ago as 1948, Harold Lasswell[2] posed a five-point approach to mass communication analysis which is good advice for listening and observing at all levels of communication:

Who
Says *what*
In which *channel*
To *whom*
With what *effect*?

I am tempted to add two crucial questions to Lasswell's list to render the analysis more comprehensive:

In what *context*
And with what *feedback*?

Of course the questions are easy to put and tantalizingly difficult to answer, especially the one seeking to discover the effect of a message upon other people. What *is* the effect a TV advertisement is having on us; is it having the same effect on other people, and which other people? If the advertisement is having different effects, what are the factors which contribute to that difference?

We listen, we observe, we investigate – that is, we gather more information, more evidence. An obvious first step is to find out whether other researches have come up with useful data in our area of investigation. We will need to locate this research evidence, note it, discuss it, check on how the information was gathered, whether the method of enquiry was valid and consider whether events have moved on from the researcher's discoveries. And ultimately, we make use of the ideas suggested by our research and that of others. We may well decide to initiate fresh lines of enquiry. To begin with, we listen and observe, then advance to more systematic means of eliciting information – document analysis, questionnaires and interviewing, see Fig. 19 overleaf.

Compiling questionnaires as a means of information gathering is standard practice in society at large and is an important skill to develop. As anyone who has tried it will tell you,

[2] In L. Bryson (ed.), 1948 *The communication of ideas* (USA: Harper and Row).

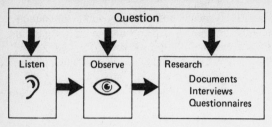

Fig. 19

putting together a questionnaire is a taxing exercise. It requires some clear thinking about exactly what information is required from people. If questions are ambiguous, the respondent will soon grow irritated. Goodwill vanishes and the questionnaire is very likely to end up in the wastepaper bin.

Good questionnaires can provide useful basic data from people in numbers, which may need to be followed up in depth by interviews. These can be a challenge to personal confidence and competence in relating to other people as well as to the capacity to formulate pertinent questions.

Interviewing requires thoughtful preparation and no interviewer should risk entering an interview without a full list of questions – though these might not all be used. If well prepared, interviews can be very enjoyable. For a start, students get out of the classroom and often out of school or college. They meet new people, of different ages, experience, knowledge, expertise and outlook.

Searching beyond the words   Interviewing can get to the heart of things because it involves chatting to people about people. You may, for example, talk to actors about their lives on the stage. You listen very carefully, not only to what is put into words, but to the hestitations, the silences – what is unsaid. And you observe, you look around you. You note the signs of that person: the arrangement of the room, the pictures on show, the books on the shelves, the clothes they are wearing.

Later, interviews have to be carefully thought about, then written up from the notes you took or the tape recordings you made of the interviews. The notes have to be sorted, their information distilled and eventually shaped into some form of address: an essay, a report, a radio programme, a video film, a play, a storyboard (sketch of each shot of a film, with notes on narrative, music and so on), a news sheet, magazine article, discussion or debate.

The skills I have listed so far can be described as enabling skills, that is they enable you to further your studies, to accumulate information upon which you will base further activity. You find out; you think out (or theorize) and finally you test out. This last stage constitutes *feedback*, for it is likely that, having conducted an investigation, you will be asked to submit your analysis, your conclusions, to those whose information, experience and ideas you have used, see Fig. 20.

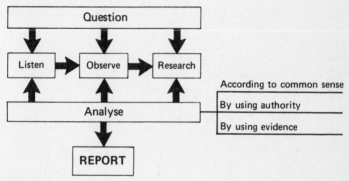

Fig. 20

The key to reporting back your findings is appropriateness: is the form of report-back appropriate to its contents and to its expected audience? Is the mode selected the one best suited to make your point with clarity and impact?

Analysing and evaluating

One of the chief values of communication studies is the emphasis it places on analysis and the rich and varied opportunities it provides for analysis. What will be analysed will obviously depend upon the particular subject matter and approach of each course. Some typical items for analysis might be: printed texts, texts with photographs, images in still and movie photography, graphical and statistical data, advertisements, sound and TV broadcasts, non-verbal communication, modes of language, dialect and accent, presentational styles (such as dress, hair, voice, manner), public speeches and theoretical models of communication.

The aim of analysis is deeper understanding. The practice of it sharpens perception which prevents students rushing into superficial judgements – that is, evaluating too early, or with insufficient evidence. It is not merely taking things apart for the sake of the exercise. Analysis should be seen as a rung on the ladder to greater appreciation of the problems and complexity of a process, and indeed towards creativity. Analysis dissects but it also builds.

How, then, do we get to grips with, say, the analysis of a situation in interpersonal communication, a TV news bulletin or a painting on the wall? We have to start somewhere and a reliable first step is to make notes. Notes are a means of activating and concentrating the mind and of ordering and simplifying material. Imaginative students may well choose to 'think with a pencil' by *drawing* ideas and facts in what is called a 'brain pattern', which represents all the relevant factors of a topic on one sheet and can be reviewed at a glance, like the one in Fig. 21 opposite.

Pictorial notes like the brain pattern here reveal the relationship between themes or ideas as they evolve. The diagram keeps a hold on one aspect of the topic while the mind searches for more. Eventually the main branches sprout minor ones – added points of information and observations.

Most analysis is initially concerned with categorizing and identifying. In Fig. 18, the politician's speech is interpersonal communication if it takes place in a church hall. It involves visible and audible group response. It takes the form both of the spoken word and non-verbal communication – gestures, movement, facial expression. Its purpose is probably to persuade and may also inform and entertain. The speech may also offend some in the audience whose views are different from those they are being subjected to. Feedback will be mixed, not easily predictable, though in the interpersonal situation John Brown MP is able to register, if he is attentive to audience reaction, how well or badly he is being received.

If the speech is being broadcast on television, it becomes mass communication. Where it gains in the size of audience, it loses in terms of effective feedback. And the speech is framed

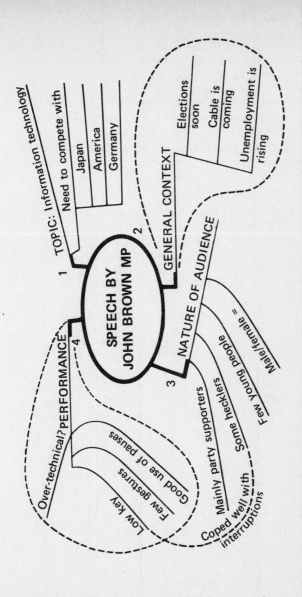

Fig. 21

within the confines of the TV screen. It is likely to have been edited down from its original length; inevitably the nature of the speech is modified.

Each text for analysis – whether it is printed, spoken, photographed, painted or broadcast – poses vital questions, and the analyst must identify what these questions are. What is the purpose of the message and how is it intended to be read by its audience? By what means – special qualities, characteristics, particulars of style and emphasis – has the message been delivered, the story told? How else could the message have been put over? Why might alternatives have been rejected?

Context   Communicative events rarely if ever happen in isolation and therefore it is most important to be aware of the context of the text. Categorizing and identifying without careful reference to context might prove misleading. Let us take two examples.

You are in the street and suddenly hear a blare of car horns. Experience might tell you that the repeated use of the horn indicates 'trouble on the road'. The signal seems angry and bullying. From clues presented to you via your ears, you turn your head expecting to see a driver bursting to overtake another who is hogging the middle of the road. However, your eyes record different evidence: you observe a line of cars each bearing white streamers from the bonnet. The context has revealed the true situation – a wedding party. Everything in our perception and response changes. By fairly common consent, wedding parties are allowed to sound a horn or two on a very special day. You may even smile and give them a wave.

On the same stroll down the street you see a lady in her garden. She is watering her flower beds with a hosepipe. She, the hosepipe, the garden, the water and you as witness, make up the text for analysis. It may seem so unimportant an event that you do not give the situation any thought. But what if there is a serious drought in the locality and the authorities have pleaded in the press for hosepipes not to be used under any circumstances?

Shifts of meaning   You may find yourself reacting to the text quite differently. You may even get so hot under the collar that you address the anti-social gardener, calling her behaviour into question. Because of the context, we may read more into the lady's behaviour than merely that of watering her garden. We may classify her attitude as being one of selfishness, of actually defying communal norms and values. In a sense, the context is *us*. We give meaning to the situation by judging it according to our own values. Of course, if you had just watered your own flower beds you might read the situation differently again – 'Good luck to her! The local authorities are panicking as usual.'

The point to be clear about here is that analysis is unlikely to lead to cut-and-dried answers. The components of communicative situations do not have the exactness of mathematical formulae. By interacting upon one another, the components charge or modify one another. For students, this means learning to cope with uncertainty. Dealing with approximations to the truth can be a lonely endeavour so it is crucial to discuss matters with others, to have one's assumptions challenged, not in a spirit of winning or losing, but through mutual exploration – listening, observing, trying out and keeping steadily aware of the context of each matter for analysis, see Fig. 22.

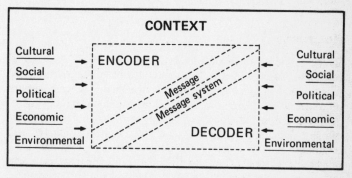

Fig. 22

Evaluation   It is not possible to separate analysis from the process of evaluation. In the first place, you have to evaluate your own analysis, test it for validity and reliability. Evaluating others should come later, but self-evaluation – of one's own work, response, performance – should be immediate and constant.

Criteria will be required for evaluation, a checklist of factors which to a greater or lesser extent will have to be fulfilled before evaluation – judgement – can reliably be said to have taken place. One important criterion for evaluation is the judgement of others. Traditionally the teacher is the chief evaluator of a student's work and performance. In communication studies there are many potential evaluators – other students, individually and in groups, friends, relatives, neighbours, topic experts; in fact, target audiences of all kinds. Their response, say to a student's film, tape-slide show or exhibition of photographs, comprises a significant part of the evaluation process, but it does not constitute the last word. The student must ultimately evaluate the evaluation, learn from it, adjust to it and even in some cases, after careful consideration, press on against the judgement of others.

Students are often extremely reluctant to pass judgement on the work of their friends in class. That, they assume, is the job of the teacher; and anyway it would be disloyal. Yet if the classroom atmosphere is warm and trusting, what educationalists call 'supportive', then constructive criticism – giving it and taking it – is a vital learning experience.

Responding

Every text for analysis and evaluation requires a personal response – an exercise in introspection, where emotional wheels and pulleys are stimulated into action. Text and self are linked in a process of discovery. This inner dialogue is intrapersonal communication (see Chapter 1). It is generated by our self-concept or self-view which has developed partly from within ourselves and partly from how other people perceive us, define us and treat us; and of course how people treat us relates to how we treat them. What we are, or how we are, conditions our way of looking on the world. It is important then for students to study themselves very carefully, to be reflective. Here are a few questions to keep close to the front of the mind:

How much have parents contributed to my self-view?
How much have school, friends, the neighbourhood, the community contributed?
How do my education, gender, social class, race, religious

denomination and my past experience of the world influence what I communicate and how?

How do other people's gender, social class, race, age, religion etc. affect my perception of what they say and do?

How do the views of parents, teachers, friends, politicians, journalists, broadcasters, writers etc. influence the way I 'read' what is going on in the world?

Reflection of this kind is more a good habit than a skill. What does constitute a skill, or a complex of skills, is the process of responding to others – getting on with them, cooperating with them, working constructively with them, understanding them. In recent years in education the terms *social skills* and *process skills* have come into regular use to describe the way we 'handle' body, mind and feelings in interpersonal relationships.

Working in groups   Probably more than in any other subject, communication studies students will find themselves working at cooperative tasks – in pairs or in groups. Such activities encourage responding skills. Whatever the task, the members of a work group are likely to learn – in the process of doing – a great deal about each other as people and about themselves in relation to others. They will learn 'how to get on'; how to adjust personal needs to the needs of the group. They will identify the different roles which a group decides it requires and adopt one which appears most suitable to their personality or their capacity to contribute to group goals, and which the group will accept.

Students working in groups will soon observe how leadership develops, that the ideas person need not always be the leader; that groups can often do very well without specified leaders. They will find themselves establishing group norms, that is, agreed ways of doing things. If the group stays together long enough, values begin to formulate – of hard work, perhaps, loyalty to group members, special care and support for the group's less able members.

All this can be invaluable experience both for the study of communication and for future life. In one way or another, most students in further or higher education will find themselves involved in committees, in work teams, in planning groups or even protest groups during and after school or college life. They will need to be familiar with the stages through which most groups pass before they become effective. One definition of these stages is:

Forming — Storming — Norming — Performing

The storming phase is what the experienced group member looks out for when a new group or a new task gets under way. After the 'we are all being polite and considerate to one another' stage of forming comes a period where people grow sufficiently in confidence to assert their individual points of view and give rein to their personalities. There are often harsh differences in the storming stage and a feeling that things are going badly, that they won't work out. An assertive personality, for example, may appear to threaten the cohesion of the group. Others may mutter about him or her being 'on an ego trip' or 'trying to batter us' with his or her opinions. For the group to pass on to the more ordered approach of the norming stage, and the creativity of the performing stage, these problems have to be tackled; hence the storming.

Responding people who have spent some time reflecting on how self comes over to others will check their performance in the light of others' disapproval. If this does not happen, the group may well turn against and even eject its awkward member. Failure to act will in any case undermine the effectiveness of the group.

Responding, then, is a facility all students must develop. It involves looking in the mirror of other people, seeing attitude and behaviour as they perceive it. It is a virtue some call *empathy*, the capacity to see things and feel things as others see and feel them.

Practising empathy   Carl Rogers[3] proposed for consideration the view that 'the major barrier to mutual interpersonal communication is our very natural tendency to judge, to evaluate, to approve (or disapprove) the statement of the other person or the other group'. Where beliefs and values are involved, that process is particularly strong. Rogers' answer is to withhold judgement and 'to see the expressed idea and attitude from the other person's point of view, to sense how it feels

[3] In *Harvard Business Review* 30, July–August 1952.

to him, to achieve his frame of reference in regard to the thing he is talking about'. He offers a rule for helping to establish such empathy: we can each speak up for ourselves only *after* we have first restated the ideas and feelings of the previous speaker accurately and to that speaker's satisfaction. It sounds simple, but Rogers warns that 'you will discover that it is one of the most difficult things you have ever tried to do'. What do you think? If this method were applied to a situation in which unions and management were locked in conflict, would it help? Some possibilities might be enough to take your breath away: if communists had faithfully to explain capitalism, and vice versa; if the *Daily Telegraph*, *Daily Express*, *Daily Mail* or the *Sun*, supporters of the Tory Party, had to explain with rational coolness the policies of the Labour Party . . .

Rogers points out how dangerous true listening might be and how it requires courage to listen rather than evaluate. Also, heightened emotions may hinder empathy. Rogers commends the importance of a 'third party, who is able to lay aside his own feelings and evaluations', and thereby 'assist greatly by listening with understanding to each person or group and clarifying the views and attitudes each holds'.

This third person may often be the teacher, but it might be useful for students in group activities to appoint such an 'observer' to referee for a while the communication process.

Applying knowledge

Communication studies is a subject in which students are expected to apply learning and at the same time to learn by application. Much work done in schools and colleges under the heading of communication skills is worthy and often useful, but it is almost always work-related. At its worst it is repetitive, mechanical and dull. One reason for this, in my view, is that skills are seen as items pegged up on a course washing line, as in Fig. 23 overleaf. I hesitate to use this cartoon because, if an image is worth a thousand words, it might stick in the mind as the right way of doing things rather than the wrong way; so let me repeat: skills and communication tasks generally which are perceived as discrete bits of clothing to be pegged up on the course programme is *not* what application is all about.

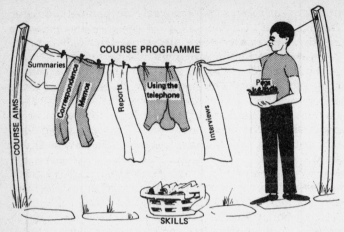

Fig. 23

If the application of knowledge, skills, competence and talent is to be meaningful it has to pass what might be called the audience test. In every case, and at every stage, we ask: Who is the message intended for? Is the mode of communication selected appropriate for that expected audience? And what evidence has been obtained to confirm the choice?

Suiting message to audience In interpersonal communication we are judging our audience all the time. Who we are talking to conditions what we say and how we say it, and not the least our motive for saying it. The information we may wish to put over to others might be to convey a good impression of ourselves; or we may want to persuade people to agree with our point of view or share our delight in something. In each case, message and delivery will be different.

If we want a favour from someone we might decide it is more appropriate to ask in person rather than use the telephone: it seems more suitable for all sorts of reasons. On the other hand, if we want a quick reply from someone in another town or company, we will probably decide the telephone is the right mode or channel to use.

Our focus is primarily the response of audience. Of course, our intention may not be to make a good impression at all. We may be out for trouble, to pick a quarrel, perhaps. *Consonance*, the amicable relationship which exists between us and our audience, gives way to *dissonance* – disturbance, distress, disagreement. As a matter of fact, few of us enjoy the feeling of dissonance. Generally we employ the means of communication to establish consonance, at least on the surface.

The difficulty comes when we aim at one and succeed in achieving the other. We can never be certain 'how we are coming over' to our audience. The mismatch between intention and effect becomes more likely the greater the number of people who constitute our audience. Thus John Brown MP addressing an election meeting hopes that his message is consonant with – at one with – the views and attitudes of the majority of the audience. The politician knows, however, that there will be an element in the audience who have come along to heckle. Their intention is to reject his message. They will very likely deliberately misread it – *aberrantly decode* the message.

Managing response through feedback   Heckling, John Brown is aware, could constitute 'noise', both technical and semantic. One answer would be to have the hecklers booted out of the hall. However, if John Brown is an experienced public speaker, and if he pays heed to the signs of audience response by careful listening and observing, he may turn the situation to his advantage, uniting the majority against the hecklers and at the same time pressing home his message more effectively than if the hecklers had not been present. He may, for example, employ knockabout humour if the mood of audience seems right for it, or he could 'fire from the hip' by underscoring the differences between 'them' (rowdy, bad mannered, ignorant) and 'us' (an attentive, supportive majority).

How John Brown fares in his speech depends on his accurate assessment of *feedback*. If clues are missed, the audience's mood misread, our politician, for all his brilliance and conviction, may fail to persuade the audience of his sincerity and authoritativeness, and his message as well as the way he has delivered it could be rejected.

In a sense, students know all about feedback. They produce work for their teachers and get high marks (positive feedback) or low marks (negative feedback). In class they might answer questions posed by the teacher which earn a nod, a smile and a compliment (positive) or a steely grimace and one of those gazes round the room which express volumes (negative).

Without feedback, communication with others is like being adrift on a night sea with neither compass nor stars to guide us. That is why listening and observing are constant priorities, and why emphasis is placed on the definition of audience for various messages and on the testing out of those messages, see Fig. 24.

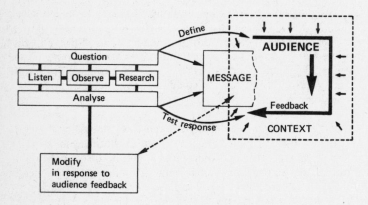

Fig. 24

Going to press One example of an application of skills, knowledge and experience which students may become involved in is the production of a magazine or newspaper. Many things can be 'learned by doing' in such a group exercise: researching, interviewing, report writing, photography, page layout; much will be learnt from working in a team; much will be learnt by accident – when things go wrong, when copy is lost, when there are holdups in processing and printing. Problems have to be discussed, possible solutions negotiated.

And then when the magazine appears, who knows? – someone may claim his or her name has been taken in vain, that information is inaccurate or misleading, style tasteless and offensive. All that is part of the process of learning, where errors and misjudgements constitute, if taken note of, points of growth. On the other hand, if the product of the exercise, the finished newspaper, is viewed as an end in itself rather than a process through which learning takes place, it might remain just another item of clothing on our course clothes line.

Focusing on the needs or requirements of an audience is a reliable way of making sure that the newspaper is more than an exercise in skills; that it is an act of communication with others. The student editorial board must constantly ask who those others are. What kind of content and style will interest them? Assuming that we cannot please all the people all the time, who do we want to please? Do we actually want to please people or would we prefer to rouse them up?

Such questions are the basis for decision-making. They give shape to editorial policy. They also help to do what Carl Rogers recommended when he suggested means of reducing barriers to communication: they oblige us to put ourselves in other people's shoes.

Antidote to stereotyping   By empathizing, we at least begin to consider that our view of things is not the only one that counts. We will avoid rushing into judgements about who our audience is, what it wants, what it can take, if we insist on *studying* what audience is, wants and can take. And this means avoiding guesses, however inspired.

The mass media have their means of measuring audience needs and responses. Nevertheless, for many reasons mass audiences remain a mystery and are often treated stereotypically: 'The Great British public prefers . . .' 'The trouble with young people these days is . . .'; Such and such a minority 'has no respect for authority . . .'

Generalizations of this kind about audience should be avoided. We must find means, in every activity, to locate and define audience and to measure feedback whether the mode of communication is a piece of writing, a film, an advertising leaflet, a poster, tape-slide show, TV programme, drama production, guidebook, shopwindow display or set of instructions.

In summary, we respond to the perceived needs of audience. In order to do this effectively we must analyse the means of communication at our disposal – its nature and characteristics – to test for appropriateness. And we never cease to monitor feedback.

Creating

I have already touched upon the importance of self-discovery in education and suggested that communication studies is a suitable vehicle for this. Unless students examine their own way of responding to self and others, what they learn will arguably be imposed from outside rather than becoming a personal commitment.

In any truly educational situation, the student, not the teacher, is the performer. If the teacher is the centre of things, then the students become the audience. Any subject worth its salt should encourage students and teachers to be both performers and audience: often they may become one in learning together.

Education is largely about self-creation. As Iredell Jenkins[4] puts it, students are their own *text*, from which a performance is created: 'I would argue that education is itself a mode of performance,' he writes, '. . . we become educated just to the degree that we become accomplished performers of ourselves'.

This takes some thinking about. Students could be forgiven for looking back on their schooling and confessing they had gained the impression that education was about passing exams in mathematics, English, geography, biology etc. In history, the text might be the Tudors, not the students studying the Tudors. Yet the longer term memory might recall those earliest school days when, as small children, students were given the chance to put a great deal more of themselves into their learning.

Personal growth   It is worth giving special emphasis to the idea that students are always at work on two texts – the script of a film, for example, and their own personal script (concerned with self definition, self esteem). The process – and the progress – of the one interacts with the process and progress of the other. That is one definition of creativity – the interaction between self and material.

Each creative task – whether it is sorting out an idea, connecting one idea with another, writing an article or a story, composing a piece of music, designing a poster, constructing a storyboard for an advertising film or organizing the sections

[4] In R.A. Smith 1970, *Aesthetic Concepts in Education* (USA: University of Illinois Press).

of a written project – poses a problem, or many problems. Creativity is about tackling problems.

Process- and person-centred and task-orientated, communication studies is also very much a problem-solving subject. When we set out on a problem we do not know, by definition, what the answer is. Finding the answer is the point of the task. We do not know where our thinking will take us. In the same way, when writers put words onto paper, or painters put paint on canvas, they rarely know exactly what will happen next.

Students entering into the open-ended tasks which constitute problems are, as I have indicated above, part of the creative process. The difference, of course, is that they are not as easily wiped clean and started again as the writer's paper or the painter's canvas. This is not tragic. It helps, though, for students to remain aware that their canvas is already marked by antecedents – by upbringing, social class, previous successes and failures; it is marked by their situation, their present position in the social and cultural environment.

An alert view of self might recognize deeply ingrained habits and attitudes on the 'canvas' which may prove to be barriers to a student's creativity.

Beating the barriers   In an amusing and stimulating tape-slide programme called *Creative thinking and brainstorming* (UK: Management Training Ltd, 1971), J.G. Rawlinson says, '. . . all of us have an innate creative ability, but the trouble is that we don't use it anything like enough'. He recommends us, in the initial stage of tackling a problem, to put aside analytical thinking, which he describes as the 'logical process of thought giving one unique and predictable answer'. We should diverge in our thinking rather than converge.

This relates back to the point about question-asking (see p. 10). We need to be working with open-ended, divergent questions rather than closed-ended, convergent ones. Below are two questions on the same topic, the first Rawlinson would classify as an analytical question, the second, a creative question:

How many national newspapers are owned by multi-national corporations?

What are the implications for the Press of multi-national ownership?

Rawlinson views creative thinking as being the product of imagination which has been given free rein. The right conditions for creative thinking are very often where individuals work in groups. Minds meet and result in sparks – if, that is, certain barriers to creativity are avoided. Rawlinson lists six such barriers. Here I will relate them to the circumstances of communication studies:

(1) The one right answer . . .

We are all of us too ready to choose the first solution to a problem which occurs to us. This applies whether we are trying to explain a person's mode of self-presentation or deciding what to do for an assignment or a project. In the first example we may, by reaching too soon for an answer, end up stereotyping a person; in the second, we may select a topic which offers us too little challenge. The answer is to go for lots of ideas; to diverge, to keep options open.

(2) The self-imposed barrier . . .

Over their school years, students may well have had – in their personal view at least – hundreds of 'bright ideas' which teachers might not have considered so bright. There is a danger that risk-taking in terms of ideas has simply not been encouraged ('Don't talk nonsense, Jones!'). Protective walls are built within which it has proved safe to operate. Creative thinking, however, involves risk-taking and expansion beyond defensive walls.

(3) Conformity . . .

There is an old saying that 'children ought to be seen and not heard'. When it comes to children's ideas or opinions about things, any number of people – parents, teachers and adults generally – might seek to impose ways of thinking upon the young which are not easily shed as children become teenagers. Conditioning of this kind is part of the process of socialization, a key area of interest. Where socialization results in an unquestioning conformity to inherited norms, values, opinions and beliefs in the developing years, growth is hindered. Rawlinson calls Barrier 3, 'giving the answer expected'.

(4) Failing to challenge the obvious . . .

In my list of vital activities for students there is no place for 'accepting'; rather, the student ought to be active in challenging the 'acceptable' which is very often presented to us in the guise of common sense; it was also common sense at one time to believe the earth was flat. It takes courage to question what all those around you consider the correct explanation of a situation, the right answer to a problem, and it requires an exercise in imagination – a creative step; assume that what everyone is telling you may not be the case.

(5) Evaluating ideas too quickly . . .

Reference was made in Chapter 1 to dualism and relativism as marking stages in a young person's maturation. Dualism, it will be remembered, describes the stage of development when things are seen in black and white, as simply correct or incorrect, right or wrong. Relativism describes an attitude which can cope with greater complexities – shades of correct and incorrect. Evaluating ideas too quickly is a tendency that, in part at least, belongs to the dualist stage. Personality, upbringing and education also contribute, of course. How often are new ideas greeted with the instant response of 'That's silly . . . that wouldn't work'? In Part 2 of his programme, *Brainstorming*, Rawlinson encourages the creative thinker to go for wild ideas, the more the better. What might at first appear a 'way out' idea, if given time to germinate and be developed, could well prove to be a winner.

(6) The fear of looking a fool . . .

No student needs this one explaining. At some time or another everyone has given an answer, voiced an opinion which has either promoted a cold shower of a response from the teacher or a gale of laughter from others in the class. Once bitten (a piece of common sense, of course) twice shy. This is a pity. Conscious of our self-image as reflected by the others in the class, we retreat into defensive communication. In future, maybe, we will keep our mouths shut. We erect a barrier which may well impede future learning and inhibit creativity.

It is important to realize that ideas never arrive fully matured. They emerge dimly, fragmentarily, hesitantly; and the products of creativity go through similarly troubled passages towards completion.

This is where working in groups can be so helpful. Once a group has learnt to delay the evaluation of ideas, it provides a supportive base from which the individual can draw confidence and take creative risks.

In writing about the ways in which people can develop their creativity, James L. Adams[5] stresses the importance of the choice of language in problem-solving. He acknowledges that education has traditionally concentrated on producing verbalizers, that is, students who are chiefly encouraged to see problems in terms of words, and that words are the medium through which important problems are solved.

Adams writes that 'Choice of the proper problem-solving language is difficult not only because the choice is usually made unconsciously, but also because of the heavy emphasis on verbal thinking (with mathematical thinking a poor second) in our culture.' He believes that, with the emphasis on verbalizing, the role of visualizing as a mode of language for problem-solving has been neglected.

Thinking pictorially   Students are often reluctant to use visualizing as a means of developing and relating ideas. Yet 'thinking with a pencil' is something all students of communication studies will find invaluable. Instead of writing it, draw it, map it, model it.

The response, 'But I can't draw' is no excuse. A talent for art is not at issue here. Indeed a facility to draw convincing portraits or landscapes may not be proof of an ability to draw ideas. Once the 'word-barrier' has been perceived by the student, thinking pictorially becomes a regular tool of analysis and creativity.

One way of rapidly developing visual perception is to engage in activities where you must reproduce things you have seen, that *make* you see. For example, Fig. 25 shows one way of drawing a conversation. This is called a sociogram, a very

[5] In *Conceptual blockbusting: a guide to better ideas* (US: W.W. Norton, 1980).

simple means of identifying the pattern of communication between persons A, B and C. The arrows indicate that A talks to B and C more frequently than C talks to B. B, in fact, says nothing to C. We might be interested in knowing why this is. If

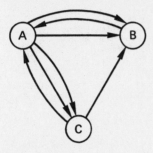

Fig. 25

we had not sketched the interaction as it happened we might not have noticed the nature of that interaction. We have arrived at the gentle art of model-making. Communication studies students will not progress far before coming into contact with conceptual models, that is, visualizations of communication processes and theory. There will be plenty of scope for students to examine some of the classic models created by thinkers whose summaries in graphic form of the complexities of human communication are the product of years of research and analysis.

Of course students will not be expected to aspire in their own modelling to the sophistication of, say, George Gerbner's model of communication in Fig. 26 (overleaf), nevertheless, students will be regularly encouraged to translate their own observations and ideas into visual form, like the simple model in Fig. 27 (overleaf), drawn by one of my own 16-year-old students, aiming to show the connection between various important elements in the communication process.

Practice in model-making will lead naturally to a familiarity with the most important conceptual models created over the years, but these are not to be regarded as prescriptive; rather they should prompt students to become 'model-makers', regularly combining observation with classification and connecting these up in visual representations.

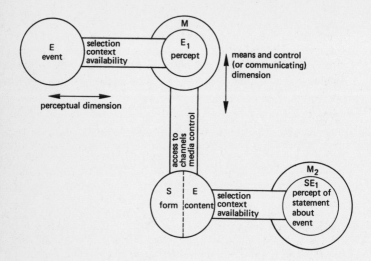

Fig. 26   A modified version of the model Gerbner presented in 'Towards a general model of communication' in *Audio Visual Communication Review*, 4.

Keep questioning   In concluding this chapter on skills and competence, I would like to stress once more the importance of question-asking, for this is the gateway to the formation of ideas, to conceptualization. As we have seen, question-asking is not always encouraged in society or even in education, for questions have the habit of challenging set ways of doing things: they upset the status quo. Yet learning is about problems, and question-asking is necessary throughout problem-solving. Without question-asking there will be little chance of ensuring a creative solution.

It is perhaps useful to point out that this mode of learning – through persistent question-asking – does not necessarily make you happy. It may even make you more discontented. If this is the case, then it should be made, in the terms of authors

Don Koberg and Jim Bagnell[6], 'constructive discontent':

> Arrival at the age of 16 is usually all that is required for
> achieving half of this important attribute of creativity. It is
> unusual to find a 'contented' young person; discontent goes
> with that time of life. To the young, everything needs
> improving . . . constructive attitudes are necessary for a
> dynamic condition; discontent is prerequisite to problem-
> solving. Combined, they define a primary quality of the
> creative problem-solver: a constantly developing Con-
> structive Discontent.

If there is truth in this statement, then it obviously helps to
retain a sense of proportion and a sense of humour.

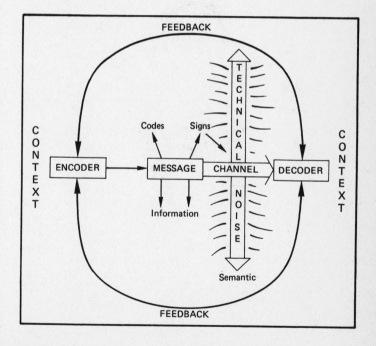

Fig. 27

[6] In *The universal traveler* (USA: Kaufman, 1974).

In Fig. 28, points about creativity are presented diagrammatically, in the form of a brain pattern. What factors would you like to add to it? Can you think of a better way of graphic presentation?

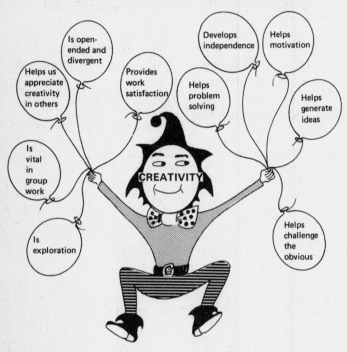

Fig. 28

5

Communication Studies: the benefits

In conclusion then, because communication studies is a boundary-crosser, it serves as an antidote to over-specialization. It bestrides a wide range of subject areas, deriving benefit from them in terms of knowledge, ideas, experience and theory. Students of communication never 'start from scratch', for they already possess a rich store of communicative experience, some of it unique, some shared currency with others. The subject obliges students to examine this experience systematically, to 'make sense of it' in wider contexts. In this way, students clarify perceptions of self and others and are likely to develop a greater understanding of the role communication plays in interpersonal and group relationships.

Communication studies seeks to transform information from master to servant. There is no fixed menu of knowledge which has to be digested before understanding can begin. Rather, communication studies places emphasis on the approach to knowledge and the handling of information in relation to the aims of study. Thus no course in communication studies can ever 'cover the syllabus' from A to Z. The possible subject-matter is too vast, too changing.

What matters is the development of means towards understanding: observation, perception, assimilation, synthesizing; and means towards doing something with that understanding: testing, evaluating, organizing and presenting, see Fig. 29.

As we have seen in Chapter 4, there are many vital skills and competences involved in communication studies, which is crucially a 'doing' subject; but the skills, like knowledge, constitute a means to understanding. They are not to be viewed as goals in themselves. The important thing is judgement – being able to decide which skills, which competences, may best serve the aim of understanding and being understood.

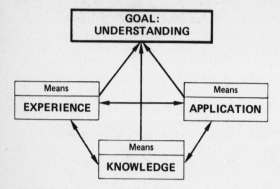

Fig. 29

We have noted how communication studies is a subject which is current: its material for study is all around us. Yet it is a subject with important historical perspectives. There is nothing to stop us visiting the ice-age caves of Lascaux or Altamira if the paintings by our ancestors cast a light on our understanding of the nature of images. We may take a trip in the imagination to the tribal lands of the Red Indian Apaches to learn something of their traditions of silence in interpersonal communication. We would most definitely be interested in the major developments in information technology, from the printing press to the telephone, from telegraphy to electronic newsgathering. Our studies may lead us into comparing modern advertising with that practised in past ages, exploring the impact of foreign travel and imperialist expansion on the English language, or the role played by silent movies in breaking through social, educational and language barriers during the early part of the twentieth century.

Escaping old constraints

Present and past, home and abroad, personal and technological – the world is our oyster because communication operates at every level in the hierarchy of human needs. It is often, for this reason, taken for granted. The study of communication attempts to reverse this complacency. In a more specific sense, it endeavours to counteract narrow definitions of what 'serious communication' is about.

In education, communication has been traditionally defined as speaking and writing, with the stress on writing. Communication studies breaks away from preoccupations with literacy. What is written down is only a fraction of the language of communication. Communication studies students are encouraged to develop skills in reading other than words – images, gestures, touch, expression, posture, body orientation, photographs, moving pictures, dance, songs, graphical data, symbols, in discriminating between what is expressed and what is meant, between what is communicated and how it is received.

A subject to enjoy

Communication studies ought also to be enjoyable as well as academically worthwhile. If you are attracted by the idea of planning and editing a newspaper, producing a radio programme, making a film, conducting an audience survey or mounting an exhibition; if you enjoy debate, creativity and working with other people, then the study of communication will be rewarding and it will be fun.

Perhaps more than in any other subject, students are expected to take their studies out of the classroom, out of school or college – interviewing people, visiting galleries, museums, film studios, broadcasting stations. It is a subject where homework can be a positive pleasure and relaxation: visits to the cinema, theatre, circus, sports stadium or fairground, to discos and parties, all constitute 'homework', that is if the student is prepared to observe and note the purposes and processes of communication. Even the most boring or unpleasant times can be put to good use. In queues at bus stops, in overcrowded trains, in the doctor's waiting room or at the outpatients' department in a hospital, observe and note.

Relevance

At its best, communication studies is 'job competent' in that it provides practice in skills essential for everyday life, from personal and social relationships to work. At the same time, the study of communication processes is of value to each and every citizen of a free and democratic society.

If we are to think independently then we must be fully aware of how communication – especially mass communication – works to confuse, to bamboozle as well as to enlighten.

As educated people we must be good 'crap-detectors', a phrase coined by Postman and Weingartner in *Teaching as a subversive activity* (Penguin, 1971), able to recognize when we are being fed misinformation and why; to distinguish reality from the construct or manufacture of reality, to spot the meaning behind the message, the ideology behind the discourse.

Like literacy and numeracy, like political and economic literacy – indeed like general education as a whole – communication studies may be deemed one of the commands of democracy. For this reason, I would argue, it should be every student's right to study the subject. Until that time comes, those who have the chance to opt for communication studies should grasp it without hesitation.

Having developed a wide knowledge of communication processes and a diverse range of communication skills, school or college leavers are equipped to approach the future with confidence. Many students, armed with an 'A' level in Communication Studies or a BTEC Diploma, go on to higher education. Others seem to be encouragingly successful in gaining a job foothold in what would appear to be the toughest areas of career opportunity – in advertising, public relations, newspapers, radio, television, information services, arts management, tourism and business generally.

One of many things they will have learnt on a communication studies course will be especially valuable: *persistence*; something learnt through project work research and simulations of real-life, work-orientated situations through case studies.

I visited all the estate agents on the High Street, hoping for information. All I got was frosty stares. I felt like running away. But I decided – I need this information, and they've got it. So I stood my ground. I went on with my quest and suddenly there was somebody willing to help. I think that experience made me a lot more determined.

This kind of experience, expressed in a student's project diary, often hurtful at the time, is invaluable when it comes to job-hunting. Communication studies students have traversed enough barriers not to be put off by unanswered letters and initially cool responses to enquiries. If letters fail, if phone calls fail, the communication studies student is likely to turn up on the doorstep, polite but determined not to take 'No' for an answer.

Appendix A: For further reading

General introductions
The following are recommended as offering a broad cultural and historical view:
J. Berger, *Ways of seeing* (Pelican, 1972).
J. Hall, *The sociology of literature* (Longman, 1979).
M. McLuhan, *The Gutenberg galaxy: the making of typographical man* (Routledge and Kegan Paul, 1962).
S.H. Steinberg, *Five hundred years of printing* (Penguin, third edition revised by James Moran, 1974).
E.S. Turner, *The shocking history of advertising* (Penguin, 1965).
R. Williams, *The long revolution* (Penguin, 1965).
R. Williams, *Television: technology and cultural form* (Fontana, 1974).
R. Williams, *Culture* (Fontana, 1981).

Compilations or readers in communication studies
These have so far been mainly orientated towards undergraduate readership; those listed below are a selection of the more introductory ones.
S. Cohen and J. Young (eds), *The manufacture of the news* (Constable, 1973).
J. Corner and J. Hawthorn (eds), *Communication studies: an introductory reader* (Edward Arnold, 1980).
J. Curran, M. Gurevitch and J. Woollacott, (eds) *Mass communication and society* (Edward Arnold, 1977).
T. Forester (ed), *The information technology revolution* (Blackwell, 1985).
G. Gumpert and R. Cathcart (eds), *Inter/media: interpersonal communication in a media world* (Oxford University Press, 1979).
M. Gurevitch, T. Bennett, J. Curran and J. Woollacott (eds), *Culture, society and the media* (Methuen, 1982).
R. Hinde, (ed), *Non-verbal communication* Cambridge University Press, 1972).

D. McQuail (ed), *Sociology of mass communications: selected readings* (Penguin, 1972).

K. Sereno and C.D. Mortensen (eds), *Foundations of communication theory* (US: Harper and Row, 1970).

Introductory textbooks on core areas of communication and media studies

J. Fiske, *Introduction to communication studies* (Methuen, 1982).

N. McKeown, *Case studies and projects in communication* (Methuen, 1982).

D. McQuail, *Communication* (Longman, 1975).

C.D. Mortensen, *Communication: the study of human interaction* (US: Mcgraw-Hill, 1972).

N. Stanton, *The business of communicating: improving communication skills* (Pan, 1982).

R. Williams, *Communications* (Penguin, 1962 and subsequent editions).

Intrapersonal and interpersonal communication

M. Argyle, *The psychology of interpersonal behaviour* (Penguin, 1972, 4th edition, 1983).

M. Argyle, *Bodily communication* (Methuen, 1975).

M. Atkinson, *Our masters' voices: the language and body language of politics* (Methuen, 1984).

D. Hargreaves, *Interpersonal relations and education* (Routledge and Kegan Paul, 1972).

E. Hall, *The hidden dimension: man's use of space in public and private* (Bodley Head, 1966).

E. Hall, *The silent language* (US: Anchor, 1973).

E. Goffman, *The presentation of self in everyday life* (Penguin, 1971 and subsequent editions).

D. Morris, *Manwatching: a field guide to human behaviour* (Cape, 1977).

M.D. Vernon, *The psychology of perception* (Penguin, 1962 and subsequent editions).

Mass communication

From the immense number of books dealing with the mass media, I consider the following to be among the most important.

D. Glover, *The sociology of the mass media* (Causeway, 1984).

R. Harris, *Gotcha! The media, the government and the Falklands* (Faber, 1983).

D. McQuail, *Mass communication theory: an introduction* (US: Sage, 1983).

D. MacShane, *Using the media: how to deal with the press, television and radio* (Pluto, 1979).

C. Seymour-Ure, *The political impact of the media* (Constable, 1974).

A. Smith, *The geopolitics of information* (Faber, 1980).

J. Tunstall, *The media in Britain* (Constable, 1983).

J. Whale, *The politics of the media* (Fontana, 1977).

Advertising

G. Dyer, *Advertising as communication* (Methuen, 1982).

V. Packard, *The hidden persuaders* (Penguin, 1960; revised and updated, 1981).

Broadcasting

D.G. Bridson, *Prospero and Ariel: the rise and fall of radio* (Gollancz, 1971).

J. Fiske and J. Hartley, *Reading television* (Methuen, 1978).

S. Hood *On television* (Pluto, 1980).

C. McArthur, *Television and history* (British Film Institute, 1978).

S. Partridge, *Not the BBC/IBA: the case for community radio* (Comedia, 1982).

R. Williams, *Television: technology and cultural form* (Fontana, 1974).

Books focusing on the analysis of news

Glasgow University Media Group, *Bad news* (Routledge and Kegan Paul, 1972); *More bad news* (Routledge and Kegan Paul, 1980); *Really bad news* (Writers and Readers, 1982).

J. Hartley, *Understanding news* (Methuen, 1982).

The press

H. Evans, *Twenty-five years through world press photos* (Quilter Press, 1981).

S. Harrison, *Poor men's guardians: a survey of the struggles for a democratic newspaper press, 1763–1973* (Lawrence and Wishart, 1974).

P. Hollis, *The pauper press* (Oxford University Press, 1970).

S. Jenkins, *Newspapers* (Faber, 1979).

A. Smith, *The newspaper: an international history* (Thames and Hudson, 1979).

D. Wainwright, *Journalism made simple* (W.H. Allen, 1972).

M. Walker, *Powers of the press; the world's great newspapers* (Quartet, 1982).

Film

E. Barnouw, *Documentary: a history of the non-fiction film* (Oxford University Press, 1974).

J. Monaco, *How to read a film* (Oxford University Press, 1977).

E. Rhode, *A history of the cinema: from its origins to 1970* (Penguin, 1976).

R. Roud (ed), *Cinema: a critical dictionary* (Secker and Warburg, 1980, 2 vols.).

B. Wright, *The long view: an international history of cinema* (Paladin, 1976).

Theatre

P. Hartnoll, *Oxford companion to the theatre* (Oxford University Press, 1983).

T. Coult and B. Kershaw (eds.) *Engineers of the imagination: the Welfare State handbook* (Methuen, 1983). A fascinating record of alternative theatre: street theatre and so on.

Technology of information

J. Graham, *Dictionary of Telecommunications* (Penguin, 1983).

R.I. Smith and B. Campbell, *Information technology revolution* (Longman, 1981).

P. Zorkoczy, *Information technology: an introduction* (Pitman, 1982).

(See also T. Forester under Compilations.)

Other general reference works

T. O'Sullivan (ed), *Key concepts in communication* (Methuen, 1983).

J. Watson and A. Hill, *A dictionary of communication and media studies* (Edward Arnold, 1984).

Useful periodicals

The Guardian runs a regular media page and generally gives thorough coverage of media activities. The BBC's *The Listener*, which appears weekly, is a lively and thoughtful magazine dealing with current broadcasting, and the weekly *New Scientist* is highly recommended for its detailed articles on aspects of information and media technology.

Other periodicals with a good record for dealing with media issues are: *New Society*, *New Statesman*, *Index on Censorship* (six issues a year) and *Media Reporter*, journal of the National Union of Journalists. The Campaign for Press and Broadcasting Freedom publishes *Free Press* as well as useful pamphlets on aspects of media performance. Film and television are comprehensively documented and analysed in *Screen*, published by the Society for Education in Film and Television, and *Sight & Sound*, journal of the British Film Institute.

Other sources
On television, Channel 4 broadcasts 'What the papers say' weekly, while on the BBC 'Panorama' and 'Horizon' often deal with issues involving mass communication. There are also plenty of programmes on radio offering valuable background on the processes and trends of mass communication. The cinema too has contributed, albeit with entertainment in mind before education, to the interpretation of media themes. Among many such films now available for hire on 16mm or video are: Lewis Milestone's *Front Page* (1930), Billy Wilder's *Ace in a Hole* (1951), Sidney Lumet's *Network* (1976), Phillip Noyce's *News Front* (1978), Roger Spottiswoode's *Under Fire* (1983) and Roland Joffe's *The Killing Fields* (1984). In 1985, the National Theatre first performed Howard Brenton and David Hare's *Pravda: a fleet street comedy*, a great theatrical success; the text of the play is published by Methuen.

Appendix B: Higher education courses in Communication and Media Studies

The Careers Research and Advisory Centre is a source of information on courses available. They publish a range of guides.

The CRAC *Degree Course Guides* give detailed comparisons of first degree courses in UK universities, polytechnics and colleges. They cover 34 individual subjects plus eight technological subjects grouped together.

CRAC *Graduate Studies* offers a comprehensive guide to postgraduate research and study facilities in the UK.

CRAC *Directory of Further Education* is the only guide to courses available at polytechnics and other institutions outside the university sector throughout the UK. It includes information on entry requirements, the standard of qualification to be obtained, the type of course and where it is available – giving full names, addresses and phone numbers of the institutions.

These guides are published by Hobsons, Ltd, Bateman Street, Cambridge CB2 1LZ and the information contained in them has been checked as carefully as possible. However, all institutions undergo changes in student numbers, staffing and research facilities and the courses on offer are thus subject to change. Intending students should ensure they consult the most recent editions, and get in touch with the institutions themselves before submitting applications.

The University Central Council on Admissions (UCCA) current *Handbook* should also be consulted.

Careers teachers at schools and the LEA Careers Guidance Officers should have these available for consultation. Many public libraries also keep copies and they are available through bookshops.

A more general book on student life and student institutions is published annually by Macmillan (Papermac), called *The Student Book*.

Other books that may be of interest are: P. Wilby, *The Sunday Times good university guide* (includes polytechnics and colleges of further education) (Granada); B. Heap, *Complete degree course offers: winning your place at university, polytechnics and other insti-*

tutions of higher education (Careers Consultants); J.K. Gilbert (ed.), *Staying the course: how to survive higher education* (Kogan Page, 1984) and *Higher education in the United Kingdom* (Longman).

Universities, polytechnics and colleges of higher education have in recent years developed an interesting range of courses centring on communication. Below is a selection.

Aston University, Gosta Green, Birmingham B4 7ET: BSc (Hons), Human Communication, with Linguistics or Philosophy, 4 years.

Bangor, Normal College of Education, Gwynedd, LL58 2DE: BA, Communications, 3 years. Competence in Welsh language desirable. Diploma in Higher Education, Communications, 2 years.

Birmingham University, PO Box 363, Birmingham B15 2TT: BA, Communication and Cultural Studies, 3 years.

Bristol Polytechnic, Coldharbour Lane, Frenchay, Bristol BS16 1QY: BA Humanities and BA (Hons), includes Communications study, 3 years.

Bulmershe College of Higher Education, Woodlands Avenue, Earley, Reading R96 1HY: BA and BA(Hons), Combined Studies includes Film and Drama, 3 years.

Canterbury Christ Church College, North Holmes Road, Canterbury, Kent CT1 1QU: BA (Hons), Radio, Film, TV Studies and Education, or Radio, Film, TV Studies and Music, 3 years.

Derbyshire College of Higher Education, Kedleston Road, Derby DE3 1GB: BA(Hons), Photographic Studies, 3 years.

Dorset Institute of Higher Education, Wallisdown Road, Wallisdown, Poole, BH12 5BB: BA and BA(Hons), English and Media Studies, 3 years.

Edge Hill College of Higher Education, St Helen's Road, Ormskirk, Lancashire L39 4QP: BA, BEd., and Diploma in Higher Education, Communication in Contemporary Society; BEd., 4 years, BA, 3 years, Dip. HE, 2 years.

Goldsmith's College, University of London, Lewisham Way, London SE14 6NW: BH and BH (Hons), Communication Studies/Education, and Communication Studies/Sociology, by course units.

Harrow College of Higher Education, Watford Road, Northwick Park, Harrow HA1 3TP: BA(Hons), Applied Photography, Film and Television, 3 years.

King Alfred's College, Winchester SQ22 4NR: BA(Hons), Drama, Theatre and Television Studies, 3 years.

Lanchester Polytechnic, Priory Street, Coventry, CV1 5FB: BA(Hons), Communication Studies, 3 years.

London College of Printing, Elephant and Castle, London SE1 6SB: BA(Hons), Photography, Film and Television, 3 years.

North Cheshire College, Fearnhead, Warrington, Cheshire WA2 0DB: BA, Media and Communication, 3 years; Dip. HE, 2 years.

Polytechnic of Central London, 309 Regent Street, London W1R 8AL: BA and BA(Hons), Film and Photographic Arts, 3 years; BA, Media Studies, 3 years.

Sheffield City Polytechnic, Pond Street, Sheffield S1 1WB: BA and BA(Hons), Communication Studies, 3 years.

Sunderland Polytechnic, Chester Road, Sunderland SR1 3SD: BA(Hons), Communication Studies, 3 years.

Trent Polytechnic, Burton Street, Nottingham N91 4BU: BA(Hons), Photography, 3 years; BA, Communication Studies, 3 years.

Trinity and all Saints' College, Brownberrie Lane, Horsforth, Leeds LS18 5HD: BA and BA(Hons), Communication Arts and Media/ Public Media, 3 and 4 years.

West Midlands College of Higher Education, Gorway, Walsall WS1 3BD: BA, Visual Communications Studies, 3 years.

New University of Ulster, Coleraine, Co. Londonderry: BA, Communication Studies, 3 years.

Ulster Polytechnic: BA, Communication Studies, 3 years.

Polytechnic of Wales, Llantwit Road, Treforest, Pontypridd Glamorgan CF37 1DL: BA, Communications and Cultural Studies, 3 years.

York, College of Ripon and York St John, Lord Mayor's Walk, YO3 7EX: BA and BA(Hons), Drama, Film and Television, 3 and 4 years.

Other courses in Communication and Media Studies
Communication in one form or another is an essential component of many school and further education courses. It is integral to the curriculum of Business and Technician Education Council (BTEC) courses, and a core element of the Certificate of Prevocational

Education (CPVE). There are also several courses run by other examining bodies, and some information on five of those is given below:

Modern Communication (O Level, Oxford University Examining Board).
Communication Studies (Mode III, Ordinary/Alternative Level, Northern Consortium; Associated Examining Board).
Communication (General Certificate of Education at Ordinary Level/Certificate of Secondary Education; Southern Consortium of Examination Boards).
Communication Skills (Level 2; City and Guilds of London Institute).
Film Study (Mode III, Ordinary/Alternative Level, Associated Examining Board, with the British Film Institute).

Appendix C: The Associated Examining Board A Level in Communication Studies

In Chapter 1, I quoted the aims of the AEB course, and while not breaking away entirely from the traditional format of A level subjects, the AEB Communication Studies has commendably shifted the emphasis of student assessment away from a rigid reliance on essay-type, unseen examinations. Paper 1 keeps to tradition: a three-hour paper with some essay work but also laying stress on the ability to analyse and interpret verbal and non-verbal texts.

It is with Papers 2 and 3 that the AEB is seen to innovate. Paper 2 is also a three-hour paper, but the Case Study material for it is provided two days before the exam. This paper sets out to test the student's ability to comprehend and handle data of all kinds, to adapt theories and models to practical situations by employing a wide range of skills. The material might be a collection of photographs, press articles, advertising handouts or business correspondence. Only when the student gets into the examination room will he or she know the exact *tasks* to be performed with the data.

In tackling Paper 2, students may be asked to prepare a story-board, write a report, summarize correspondence, do a press handout, write a radio, TV or talk script, etc. The paper tests the ability to absorb and synthesize material and to shape this material in appropriate forms for a clearly defined audience or readership.

Project work

Paper 3 constitutes a major project which has to be submitted in early spring, prior to the final examination (Papers 1 and 2) in the summer. The Project can take many forms – extended reports, handbooks, guidebooks, radio programmes, video or cine-films, tape-slide shows, dramatic performances, exhibitions, etc. The Project is designed to nurture independent learning, research skills and the ability to organize and present material.

Students must make sure not only that they have a clear picture of the audience for which the Project is intended but provide evidence that there *is* an audience for their work, and that the mode of communication selected is appropriate for that audience. They must be prepared to test out the idea for the Project prior to getting under way, and are advised to keep checking where possible throughout the exercise. The finished product must then be submitted for direct scrutiny by a selection of the proposed audience – using questionnaires, perhaps, or interviewing – and the audience response written up and analysed. This analysis is submitted for assessment with the Project, along with a *Diary* or *Log* which students are expected to keep from the moment they first consider what project to do, and how.

The Project is rounded off with an oral assessment which carries 10 per cent of the overall marks. Further details can be obtained from the AEB guide notes.

A typical case study

Below is an example of the kind of assignment A level Communication Studies students will be expected to tackle. It is taken from an AEB Paper 2, Case Study.

Two days before the exam, students received the following documents:

1 A letter from Chorlton Careers Service to the Personnel Officer of Glossop Cranes and Gears, who regularly take on school leavers. The letter included statements made about the firm's interviewers by past interviewers (for example 'There was this one, younger bloke, who was OK. He seemed quite interested in me. Asked me about hobbies. But the rest couldn't wait to get rid of me.', 'I felt a real fool. All I could think of to say was "Yes" or "No". They must have thought I was really stupid.', 'There was this one who kept staring at me. I felt so nervous. Didn't know where to look. Most of them were all right, though. About what I expected.', 'There was one chap who thought he was really smart. He kept asking me stupid questions, trying to catch me out.', 'It was an enormous room, they all sat behind a big, old table and I had to sit on a chair, miles away, in front of them, wish I'd had a table to lean on, too!').

2 A briefing sheet on the character of the crane company Training Manager (for example, 'When you try interviewing them, it's amazing: there seems to be no relationship between the academic results, the school reports and the youths I see in front of me. Some of them don't even wear a tie, let alone a suit, and they positively flaunt their earrings at me. Some of them don't seem to have an opinion of their own – it's all "y'know" and "all right" – and the only interests they profess are in the most powerful noisy motorbikes they can find and the latest skiffle groups I've never heard of. The rest of them are all question, question – and no appreciation of the need to make

profits to keep the company going. One of them, the other week, lit up a cigarette in the middle of the interview – at least he had the politeness to ask if he could and I was so taken aback I'd said yes before I could think of anything else. Then he goes on to challenge me as to whether we do anything socially useful as a company and next thing he's asking me why we had to make 200 workers redundant last year! And his school report said he was a mature young man intellectually capable of grasping a complex argument!').

3 A letter from the crane company commissioning a video for their training programme, to include contrast between effective and ineffective styles of interviewing, making use of the character sketch mentioned in document 2 above, and a set of 'commandments' for interviewing technique (for example, 'Be on your guard against your own prejudices – you may not like the candidate's appearance and opinions, but he may have a lively mind and the skills you are looking for.', 'Speak slowly and distinctly, but don't treat the candidate like a simpleton – the good candidate will always respond to searching questions, if they're sympathetically put.', 'The closed question will not help you to discover what you need; the open question may reveal hidden gold.', 'Remember it's an interview you're conducting, not an inquisition, so think about the lighting and the arrangement of the furniture.', 'Do not interrupt a candidate in the middle of an answer unless you have a very good reason to do so. Think about how you feel when someone interrupts you.'). The video should also emphasize listening and non-verbal communication. The letter also requested a design for a form for management staff to fill in during their second viewing of the video.

Students then had two days to read and absorb the documents, and to consider what tasks would be based upon the material. The exam paper itself, allowing three hours, sets the scene:

You have been appointed as a production assistant at a small communications consultancy. Your producer is away on holiday and you have been asked by your director to respond to the commission in your boss's absence.

Task One: Write a script with visual instructions for a ten-minute video which will demonstrate and highlight the need for a range of effective interviewing skills.

(script: 35 marks)
(visual instructions: 35 marks)

Task Two: Produce an observer's sheet (text and layout) to help focus discussion upon specific aspects of the video and of interviewing skills. The sheet will be completed by managers during their second viewing of the video.

(30 marks)

Index